The Journal of Andrew Fuller Studies 8
Published in the United States of America
by The Andrew Fuller Center for Baptist Studies
The Southern Baptist Theological Seminary
2825 Lexington Road
Louisville, Kentucky 40280

© The Andrew Fuller Center for Baptist Studies 2024

All rights reserved. No part of this publication may be reproduced, stored in a retrieval system, or transmitted, in any form or by any means, without the prior permission in writing of The Andrew Fuller Center for Baptist Studies, or as expressly permitted by law, by license, or under terms agreed with the appropriate reproduction rights organization.

ISBN 978-1-77484-156-3

Printed by H&E Publishing, West Lorne, Ontario, Canada

The Journal of Andrew Fuller Studies

The Journal of Andrew Fuller Studies is an open access, double-blind peer-reviewed, scholarly journal published online biannually in the Spring and Fall by the Andrew Fuller Center for Baptist Studies (under the auspices of The Southern Baptist Theological Seminary). The publication language of the journal is English. Articles that deal with the life, ministry, and thought of the Baptist pastor-theologian Andrew Fuller are very welcome, as well as essays on his friends, his Particular Baptist community in the long eighteenth century (1680s-1830s), and the global impact of his thought, known as "Fullerism."

Articles and book reviews are to follow generally the style of Kate L. Turabian, *A Manual for Writers of Research Papers, Theses, and Dissertations*, 9th ed. (Chicago, IL: University of Chicago Press, 2018). They may be submitted in British, American, Australian, New Zealand, or Canadian English. Articles should be between 5,000 and 8,000 words, excluding footnotes. Articles are to be sent to the Editor and book reviews to the Book Review Editor.

Editor:
Michael A G Haykin, ThD, FRHistS
Professor of Church History
& Director, The Andrew Fuller Center for Baptist Studies
The Southern Baptist Theological Seminary, Louisville, Kentucky
mhaykin@sbts.edu

Associate editor:
Baiyu Andrew Song, PhD, FRAS
Adjunct Course Professor
Carey Theological College
Vancouver, BC
basong@carey-edu.ca

Design editor & Book review editor:
Caleb Anthony Neel, PhD cand.
The Southern Baptist Theological Seminary, Louisville, Kentucky
cneel@sbts.edu

Editorial board:
Cindy Aalders, DPhil
Director of the John Richard Allison Library
& Assistant Professor of the History of Christianity
Regent College, Vancouver

Dustin B. Bruce, PhD
Dean & Assistant Professor of Christian Theology and Church History
Boyce College
Louisville, Kentucky

Chris W. Crocker, PhD
Pastor, Markdale Baptist Church, ON
& Associate Professor of Church History
Toronto Baptist Seminary
Toronto, Ontario

Chris Chun, PhD
Professor of Church History & Director of the Jonathan Edwards Center
Gateway Seminary
Ontario, California

Jenny-Lyn de Klerk, PhD
Editor, Book Division
Crossway
Wheaton, Illinois

Jason G. Duesing, PhD
Provost & Professor of Historical Theology
Midwestern Baptist Theological Seminary
Kansas City, Missouri

Nathan A. Finn, PhD
Provost & Dean of the University Faculty
North Greenville University
Tigerville, South Carolina

C. Ryan Griffith, PhD
Pastor, Cities Church
St. Paul, Minnesota

Peter J. Morden, PhD
Principal
Bristol Baptist College
Clifton Down
Bristol, England

Adriaan C. Neele, PhD
Director, Doctoral Program & Professor of Historical Theology
Puritan Reformed Theological Seminary
Grand Rapids, Michigan
& Research Scholar
Yale University, Jonathan Edwards Center
New Haven, Connecticut

Robert Strivens, PhD
Pastor, Bradford on Avon Baptist Church (UK)
& Lecturer in Church History
London Seminary
London, England

Tom Nettles, PhD
Senior Professor of Historical Theology
The Southern Baptist Theological Seminary
Louisville, Kentucky

Blair Waddell, PhD
Pastor, Providence Baptist Church
Huntsville, Alabama

Contents

The Journal of Andrew Fuller Studies
No. 9, Fall 2024

Editorial
Bicentenary Anniversary of William Ward's Death — 9
Michael A.G. Haykin

Portrait of William Ward — 11

Articles
Written on a heart of flesh: The Life of William Ward — 12
Caleb Hawkins, Landen Llamas, Joshua Sherrell, and Matthew Stewart

Portrait of William Ward — 18

More than a printer: The many roles of William Ward in the Serampore Mission — 19
Matthew Marvin Reynolds

Photo of William Ward's Statue in Serampore — 36

Providence and pragmatism: Early societal engagement of the Serampore missionaries — 37
Peter de Vries

The Serampore mission and the Moravian connection — 55
Samuel E. Masters

Texts & documents
The Form of Agreement — 69
William Ward

William Ward Bibliography — 78
Caleb Hawkins, Landen Llamas, Joshua Sherrell, and Matthew Stewart

Photo of William Ward's Grave in Serampore — 81

Editorial: Bicentenary Anniversary of William Ward's Death

Michael A.G. Haykin

Michael A.G. Haykin is Chair and Professor of Church History and Director, The Andrew Fuller Center for Baptist Studies at The Southern Baptist Theological Seminary, Louisville, KY.

March 17, 2023, marked the bicentenary of the death of William Ward (1769–1823), a Baptist missionary who, as a partner of William Carey (1761–1834), played a crucial role in the birth of modern missions. He would be much better known had he not labored in the shadow of Carey.

Ward was responsible for printing the Bible in numerous languages of India, including Tamil, Bengali, and Marathi. He managed a printing enterprise that functioned on an industrial scale. Over seventy people, including Muslims and Hindus, worked together to produce paper and ink for the Serampore community, fabricate type in various languages, and print an endless stream of books, dictionaries, tracts, newspapers, and Bibles.

Ward began as a journalist involved in radical politics in England before being recruited to print Bibles at Serampore. In India, he helped establish pioneering periodical publications in English and Bengali. Ward maintained his interest in social issues but made the preaching of the cross the focal point of his life. And he produced one of the first ethnographic investigations of India, a massive study initially published in four volumes. He also wrote a biography of Krishna Pal, the first Hindu convert baptized by the Serampore missionaries, and other works of a devotional nature.

His most enduring legacy might be the Serampore Form of Agreement (SFA), which is reproduced in this issue of *The Journal of Andrew Fuller Studies*. Composed by Ward, the Serampore missionaries signed this covenant in 1805. While some aspects of the SFA are dated, it remains one the most valuable missiological manuals ever produced, and its timeless principles are relevant for contemporary missions.

The papers by Matthew Reyonolds,. Peter de Vries, and Sam Masters were all part of the bicentennial celebration of Ward's life held at The Southern Baptist Theological Seminary under the auspices of *The Andrew Fuller Center for Baptist Studies* in December of 2023. The first article, co-written by four doctoral students at Southern Seminary had its origins in a doctoral seminar that I led on 18th-century English Baptist thought and piety at Southern Seminary in the final week of November of last year. Due to the size of this issue, we have decided to defer including our customary book reviews till the next issue in the spring of 2025.

Written on a heart of flesh: The Life of William Ward

Caleb Hawkins, Landen Llamas, Joshua Sherrell, and Matthew Stewart

Caleb Hawkins is a pastor at Generations Church in Norcross, GA, who also serves as the managing editor for Hanover Press. Landen Llamas is a missionary in the Czech Republic and is a member of the Baptist Church in Olomouc, CZ, where he serves among the youth. Joshua Sherrell is the Associate Pastor at Providence Church of Lehigh Acres, FL. Matthew Stewart serves as VP of Academic Affairs at Cross Theological Seminary in Rogers, Arkansas. All four men are currently pursuing PhDs in Historical and Theological Studies from The Southern Baptist Theological Seminary.

What would modern missions be without William Carey (1761–1834)? What would William Carey be without William Ward (1769–1823)? Ward's place in the pioneering work of global missions has been dimmed by the spotlighting of Carey in the history of Christian missions. Yet a full picture of the tales of God's work in eighteenth- and nineteenth-century India cannot be told without acknowledging the buttress Ward was in those endeavors. Carey was certainly the "mission's patriarch, around whom many other Baptist missionaries found their place," but without Ward, Carey would not have accomplished all he did.[1]

Biographical Sketch: Ward in England
In Derby, England, William Ward was born on October 20, 1769. His mother's name is not recorded, though some have claimed to identify her.[2] His father, John, was a carpenter who died during William's childhood. After completing his schooling, Ward became an apprentice to John Drewry (1739–1794), a printer and bookseller in Derby.[3] His skills blossomed and he was rewarded with growing responsibilities as editor of multiple newspapers owned by Drewry.[4] Ward's mastery of typesetting and editing would greatly

---

[1] A. Christopher Smith, "The Legacy of William Ward and Joshua and Hannah Marshman," *International Bulletin of Missionary Research* 23, no. 3 (1999): 120. Joshua Marshman is also a vital figure to include in this discussion as the third member of the "Serampore Trio." Smith goes on to write, "Ward and the Marshmans freed him [Carey] up in a unique way to engage in a specialized ministry that gained public acclaim" (Smith, "The Legacy of William Ward," 120).

[2] Matthew Reynolds, "The Spirituality of William Ward" (PhD diss, The Southern Baptist Theological Seminary, 2019), 22.

[3] Reynolds, "Spirituality of William Ward," 23.

[4] Smith, "Legacy of William Ward," 120.

benefit his later missionary work. Alongside his professional life was his engagement in social activism. He stemmed from the Methodist tradition and sympathized with the mistreatment of the "dissenters" by the government; his involvement with the cause of dissenters put him legal and professional peril at times.[5]

By 1791, Ward worked his way up to the role of editor at the *Derby Mercury* and later became the editor at the British newspaper, *Hull Advertiser and Exchange Gazette*.[6] As Ward applied himself to his craft, he became a capable editor and could have had a lucrative career in the printing business. Speaking of Ward's abilities, Stennett stated, "Thus was he early initiated into public life, nor was he by any means ill-qualified for the part he had undertaken. A mind naturally aspiring ... an ardent imagination, a lively wit, united to a tolerably discriminating judgment of men and things, made him a valuable assistant in the conducting of a provincial journal."[7]

While working as an editor, Ward continued to show interest in political issues. In 1791, he helped found the Derby Society for Political Information (SPI), which consisted of middle-class industrialists and professionals who came together to work on local improvement committees.[8] Ward was asked to draw an "Address declaratory of their principles" for the group's first public meeting on July 16th, 1792.[9] The address called for reforms in the government and was eventually printed in London's *Morning Chronicle* on Christmas Day, and it caused quite a stir. The editor of the *Morning Chronicle*, James Perry (1756–1821), was prosecuted for printing the address which was seen as having a seditious tone and was narrowly acquitted.[10] At this time, Ward had his first interactions with the Baptists. As a child, Ward grew up going to Methodist meetings with his mother and developed a strong connection to the Christian faith. However, at some point in 1791, he made his first connections with the Particular Baptists and started to change his theological convictions.[11] It was in Derby that he began to regularly attend services at the Baptist church and would even attend Baptist meetings in the neighborhood.[12] However, he did not receive baptism until several years later. Stennett records:

> It does not appear, however, that he made a public profession of his faith before his removal to Hull, which took place about the year 1794 or 1795. Here he fell in with a Baptist Church, meeting in Salt-House land under the pastoral care of the late Mr. [John] Beatson [1743–1798], and after some time, was baptized by him, and joined the church, of which he continued as an honourable and useful member during his

---

5 Christopher A. Smith, "William Ward, Radical Reform, and Missions in the 1970s," *American Baptist Quarterly* 10, no. 3 (1991): 222–30.

6 Reynolds, "Spirituality of William Ward," 24–25.

7 Samuel Stennett, *Memoirs of the Life of the Rev. William Ward, Late Baptist Missionary in India; Containing a Few of His Early Poetical Productions, and Monody to His Memory* (London: Simpkin and Marshall, 1825), 11.

8 Smith, "William Ward, Radical Reform," 224–225.

9 Smith, "William Ward, Radical Reform," 226.

10 Reynolds, "Spirituality of William Ward," 26–27.

11 Reynolds, "Spirituality of William Ward," 28.

12 Reynolds, "Spirituality of William Ward," 28.

residence in that town.[13]

Ward's faithful service in the local church gained the attention of church leaders and of Richard Fishwick (1745–1825) of Newcastle-upon-Tyne, a man of great wealth.[14] It was through this connection that Ward was able to receive funding to devote himself completely to the preparation for gospel ministry. Ward accepted the offer and decided to embark on a completely new career path. We get a glimpse into Ward's frame of mind after accepting the call to full time ministry in a letter written to a friend dated July 20, 1797, in which Ward wrote: "I thought I had been fixed at Hull … I was surrounded by friends, on whose smiles I sometimes imprudently fed. My mind was calm, and I had some leisure for my friend and my books … In the midst of these employments and pleasures, I received an invitation to go to Ewood Hall––to leave Hull––perhaps forever!! Conscience commands me to go––to enter on a new line of life."[15] Ward seemed to embrace this new calling with a simple faith and a resolute determination.

With his calling confirmed and his expenses paid, Ward headed off to study theology at Ewood Hall, Hebden Bridge, near Halifax, in the west riding of Yorkshire, to prepare for ministry under the tutelage of John Fawcett (1740–1817).[16] Fawcett came to faith at a young age during the time of the Great Awakening in England and he was converted through the preaching of George Whitefield (1714–1770).[17] He was ordained in 1765 and became one of the most significant Baptists of his day.[18] It was under Fawcett, Ward spent over a year learning theology and the biblical languages.

Besides putting his time to study, Ward also preached to different congregations around the school. In fact, Ward took any opportunity available to preach and became known for being willing to travel great distances to teach in small gatherings. Sharing the story of one such occasion where Ward was preaching to a group of believers in an old cottage, Stennett recorded that "There, elevated on a three-legged stool, with his little Bible in his hand, did he often preach, with fervour and affection, the unsearchable riches of Christ to an audience crowded to the full extent of the little cottage-room, in which it was assembled. It was in these meetings, that his missionary zeal seems to have been kindled."[19]

It was also during his time at Ewood Hall, Ward met committee members of the Baptist Missionary Society (BMS).[20] These interactions had a strong impact on Ward and he wrote a letter to Andrew Fuller (1754–1815), the secretary of BMS.[21] In return, Fuller

---

13 Stennett, *Memoirs of the Life of the Rev. William Ward*, 14.

14 Reynolds, "Spirituality of William Ward," 30. On Fishwick, also see Baiyu Andrew Song, "'The Steady Obedience of His Church': The Ecclesial Spirituality of Joseph Kinghorn and the Communion Controversy, 1814–1827" (PhD diss., The Southern Baptist Theological Seminary, 2023), 38–43.

15 Stennett, *Memoirs of the Life of the Rev. William Ward*, 32–33.

16 Stennett, *Memoirs of the Life of the Rev. William Ward*, 34.

17 Reynolds, "Spirituality of William Ward," 32.

18 Reynolds, "Spirituality of William Ward," 33.

19 Stennett, *Memoirs of the Life of the Rev. William Ward*, 39–40.

20 Reynolds, "Spirituality of William Ward," 35.

21 Smith, "Legacy of William Ward," 121.

invited Ward to the next BMS meeting at Kettering in October of 1798 and preach to the group. His preaching and interview were well received, and he was accepted as one of their missionaries.[22] We get a picture into his understanding of his missionary call in a response he wrote to Fuller, who asked him about his motives for going into ministry. Ward responded:

> I have received no new revelation on the subject; I did not expect any. Our Redeemer has said, Go ye into all the world, and preach the gospel to every creature: and lo, I am with you always, even to the end of the world. This command I consider as still binding; since the promise of Christ's presence reaches to the utmost corner of the earth, and to the utmost boundaries of time.[23]

Ward, thus, carried such a conviction into the next season of his ministry. He finished his training and became ready to embark on a journey that would take him halfway around the world.

Biographical Sketch: Ward in India
In May of 1799, Ward was set apart for the work of missions by the BMS. Seventeen days later, Ward boarded a ship set for India with fellow missionaries including Joshua Marshman, and his future wife, Mary Tidd Fountain (1773–1832). His homeland became Ward's background, and his heavenly harvest was a sea voyage away. The vessel of missionaries arrived in India on the Lord's Day, October 13, 1799.[24] It seems that they made mistakes by being too forward about their missionary purposes and brought heat upon themselves from British officials as they made their way into indigenous territory.[25] They fled to Serampore and settled there. Later, Ward was sent to convince Carey and his family to relocate to Serampore.[26]

The band of missionaries established the Mission and constituted their church soon after Carey's arrival on April 24, 1800.[27] Thus began Ward's ministry from Serampore, where called home for the rest of his life. As for family life, Ward married the widow of John Fountain, Mary Tidd, in 1802, and adopted her son.[28] William and Mary late had four daughters, but only two of them survived adulthood. A sorrowful chapter of Ward's life involved a fire in 1812 that burned up the print shop along with the loss of his daughter

---

[22] Stennett, *Memoirs of the Life of the Rev. William Ward*, 49.

[23] Stennett, *Memoirs of the Life of the Rev. William Ward*, 61–62.

[24] Reynolds, "Spirituality of William Ward," 37–38; A month into the voyage, Ward wrote of his ambitions: "Blessed be God that I have seen this land and that I am now on board a vessel, which will, I trust, carry me to India, to print the New Testament. 'Unto me, who am less than the least of all saints, is this grace given, that I should [print] amongst the Millions in India, the unsearchable riches of Xt'" (William Ward, Journal MSS, Lord's Day, May 26, 1799, 1, as quoted in Reynolds, "Spirituality of William Ward," 37–38).

[25] Smith, "Legacy of William Ward," 122.

[26] Reynolds, "Spirituality of William Ward," 41.

[27] Reynolds, "Spirituality of William Ward," 42.

[28] Reynolds, "Spirituality of William Ward," 64; Ward desired his wife and other sisters of the mission to be co-laborers of the gospel. He wrote: "I cannot bear that our sisters should be mere house-wives" (Ward, Journal MSS, Tuesday, May 25 [26], 1807, 550, as quoted in Reynolds, "Spirituality of William Ward," 64).

around this time as well.²⁹

In the church, Ward first served as a deacon and became a co-pastor with Marshman and Carey in 1805. In the Serampore Mission, Ward was a pillar of so many areas. Reynolds identifies a plethora of roles Ward fulfilled, including printer, preacher, evangelist, mentor, mission administrator, missiologist, theologian, historian, draftsman, author, college professor, pastor, husband, father, counselor, peacemaker, and friend.³⁰ His printing skills and management of the printing operation stood out. His publishing launched "paper missionaries" across the region.³¹ Many thousands of texts were produced under his watch, including Bible translations, tracts, dictionaries, books, Hindu texts, among others.³² By the end of his life, Ward's printing outpost at Serampore included nineteen presses and over two hundred employees.³³

Though his work as a printer was outstanding, his other contributions to the missionary cause could not be overlooked. He was a passionate evangelist and mentor of indigenous converts for the purpose of sending them out as an effective means of evangelization among their own people.³⁴ Effective preaching in various contexts amongst the agglomeration of European and Asian peoples present in the region was also a great strength.³⁵ His own publications were also impressive.³⁶ The first edition of his groundbreaking four-volume study of Hinduism entitled, *A View of the History, Literature, and Mythology of the Hindoos: Including A Minute Description of Their Manners and Customs, And Translations From Their Principal Works*, appeared in 1806.³⁷ This enormous work reflects the Serampore Trio's commitment to "missionaries coming to terms with Indian culture."³⁸ Another important document Ward drafted was the *Serampore Form of Agreement*, which was published in 1805.³⁹ This text contained the governance of the Mission along

---

29 He explained his inner thoughts to a friend in a letter and wrote, "Notwithstanding this loss by the fire so great, I felt much more for the loss of my dear child, than for this; she was a charming child, and had entwined herself round my heart so much, that I seem never to have seen affliction till this child was taken from me. I had never calculated on the death of any of my family; but had always been thinking of being taken from them ... I have now two daughters left, and Mrs. Ward's son by Mr. Fountain ... I have many comforts left, and am very happy in my family; but I much wish to see the work of grace begun in the hearts of my children, before I go hence" (Stennett, *Memoirs of the Life of the Rev. William Ward*, 176–77).

30 Reynolds, "Spirituality of William Ward," 43.

31 J. Ryan West, "Evangelizing Bengali Muslims, 1793–1813: William Carey, William Ward, and Islam" (PhD diss., The Southern Baptist Theological Seminary, 2014), 236–37.

32 Reynolds, "Spirituality of William Ward," 49.

33 Stennett, *Memoirs of the Life of the Rev. William Ward*, 183.

34 Reynolds, "Spirituality of William Ward," 52.

35 Reynolds, "Spirituality of William Ward," 47.

36 For a full listing and review of Ward's published works and unpublished material, see Reynolds, "Spirituality of William Ward," 8–16.

37 William Ward, *A View of the History, Literature, and Religion of the Hindoos: Including A Minute Description of Their Manners and Customs, And Translations From Their Principal Works*, In Two Volumes, 2nd ed. (Serampore: Mission Press, 1815).

38 Smith, "Legacy of William Ward," 126.

39 The document was reprinted in [Ernest Payne], "The Serampore Form of Agreement," *Baptist Quarterly* 12, no. 5 (1947): 125–38.

with detailing the central doctrine and philosophy of ministry amongst the Serampore Trio.

After spending his years in Serampore, Ward developed troubling stomach maladies and was persuaded by trusted friends to return to England for some relief in 1819.[40] Yet Ward did not take such a trip as a holiday. He wrote a year-long devotional for publication *en route* to England and travelled to the United States and the Netherlands on behalf of the Baptist Mission.[41] His health was somewhat rejuvenated, but Ward was more encouraged by the money he raised for the Mission's new college, of which Ward was administrator.[42] His return to the expanding Serampore Mission in 1821 was much needed as Ward was so depended upon to keep many of its parts moving.[43] This made his death quite a blow to the work in Serampore and beyond. After a short but dire battle with cholera, William Ward entered the joy of his Lord on March 7, 1823.[44] The significance of Ward's life and work was recognized in his brothers' doubts that they could go on without him. At his funeral, Marshman confessed, "Our beloved brother was so endeared to us in every capacity, that had our feelings been consulted, we should never have suffered him to enter into rest but with ourselves."[45]

---

40 Smith, "Legacy of William Ward," 126–27.

41 William Ward, *Reflections on The Word of God For Every Day In The Year* (Serampore: Mission Press, 1822).

42 Reynolds, "Spirituality of William Ward," 66.

43 Reynolds, "Spirituality of William Ward," 67.

44 Reynolds, "Spirituality of William Ward," 67.

45 Stennett, *Memoirs of the Life of the Rev. William Ward*, 230–1.

More than a printer:
The many roles of William Ward in the Serampore Mission

Matthew Marvin Reynolds

Matthew Reynolds previously served overseas in the area where the Serampore Trio served over two hundred years ago and now serves as director of Refuge International in Louisville, Kentucky.

Though the primary contribution envisioned for William Ward was in printing, he came, in time, to fill many vital roles in and beyond the Serampore Mission. Others have recognized that Ward "served with distinction as [a] peacemaker, personnel manager, pastoral counselor and publisher," that he devoted himself to "the training for missionary duties, of the advanced youth in the college," and that Carey himself "relied on William Ward to maintain the vital psychological middle ground in his team."[1] An even more comprehensive list includes the roles of preacher, evangelist, mentor, mission administrator, missiologist, theologian, historian, draftsman, author, college professor, pastor, husband, father, counselor, peacemaker, and friend. At first glance, this grouping of roles might appear random and unconnected. Upon closer examination, these roles are intimately connected with specific core threads of Ward's spirituality including love, humility, prayer, and usefulness. Considering these roles reveals that Ward was much more than a mere printer; it reveals why Ward became indispensable to the Serampore Mission and was greatly loved by all who knew him.

Printer
Though Ward felt most in the line of duty while itinerating, and, received the warmest approbation in connection with roles yet to be discussed, Ward's "9 to 5" routine was in the print shop.[2] A glimpse at the mundane nature of this work is seen in the following:

> *Wednesday, July 1st, 1808*—Translated for my book till night. After worship in the

---

[1] A. Christopher Smith, *The Serampore Mission Enterprise* (Bangalore, India: Centre for Contemporary Christianity, 2006), 24, 81; Helen H. Holcomb, *Men of Might in India Mission* (New York: Fleming H. Revell, 1901), 89.

[2] Of his itinerancy in Dinagepore, Ward wrote on Wednesday, October 5, 1803: "Perhaps in all these labours we are casting bread on the waters, which will not be seen till after many days,, but I never felt myself more in the path of duty" (William Ward, *BMS Missionary Correspondence; William Ward; Transcript of Diaries in 2 Books Comprising 4 Volumes; Book 1 [Vols. 1 & 2] 1799–1805; Book 2 [Vols. 3 & 4] 1806–1811* [London: Baptist Missionary Society Archives, 1981], 332).

> office, settled a number of accounts, & c. and examined a proof in Orissa. After dinner attended office business & read two proofs of my books—journalized, & ca. *Wednesday, July 2nd, 1808*—Translated for my book before breakfast—attended to Persian exercise—read a Bible proof; translated for my book till ten; read another of my proofs.[3]

Though mundane, the work of the press was part of the Mission's core strategy.[4] It was at the Mission Press that Ward published tens of thousands of tracts and pamphlets, grammars, dictionaries, Hindu works, original works, and of course, numerous translations of the Bible into various Indian languages.[5] Once published, the tracts and Scriptures became "paper missionaries" in the hands of BMS and national missionaries alike.[6] The following entry from Ward's *Journal* shows the typical role of the press in mission outings.

> This forenoon we had about 30 people from different villages ... They sat down in my room, & Presad talked excellently to them. Rotton said a little. We then sung; after which I talked. Before they broke up we gave each one a tract, & to three of them we gave the Scriptures, two testaments & one old testament. Others wanted the Scriptures, but we had none to give them.[7]

The white foreigner and literature in their own tongue was often the initial draw, but it was through the testimony of men like themselves—former Hindus who had renounced their caste—that new converts were made.[8] Over time, a steady stream of enquirers began to make their way to Serampore to learn more about what they had read in the tracts and Scriptures. Those that had serious impressions were considered for baptism, and those that weren't returned to their homes.[9]

In addition to its missiological role, the press also served as an alternating source of contention and pacification about the British government while providing the Mission with much needed revenue. The press was contentious because of its potential to agitate

---

[3] Ward, Journal MSS, Wednesday, July 2nd, 1808, 662.

[4] In an address Ward drew up for the British public in 1819 on his voyage to England, he set forth three departments of labor which had existed since the beginning of the Serampore Mission, *viz.*, preaching, translation, and schools. All members at different times and to varying degrees and ways, participated in the first two labors, while their labor in schools was under the care of John and Hannah Marshman. Part of the reason for Ward's return to England was to raise support for a new, fourth labor of the Mission, in the establishment of a college, "intended chiefly for the instruction of native teachers and pastors in secular and Christian knowledge" (*The Life and Times of Carey, Marshman and Ward* [1859; repr., Serampore: Council of Serampore College, 2005], 2:197).

[5] Stennett mentions that Ward "carrying through the press not less than *twenty* translations of the Holy Scriptures into the languages of the East" (Samuel Stennett, *Memoirs of the Life of the Rev. William Ward, Late Baptist Missionary in India; Containing a Few of His Early Poetical Productions, and a Monody to His Memory* [London: Simpkin and Marshall, 1825], 95).

[6] J. Ryan West, "Evangelizing Bengali Muslims, 1793-1813: William Carey, William Ward, and Islam" (PhD diss., The Southern Baptist Theological Seminary, 2014), 236-37.

[7] Ward, Journal MSS, Saturday, October 22nd, 1803, 339.

[8] Ward, Journal MSS, Lord's Day, April 19th, 1801, 151; Tuesday, October 13th, 1801, 175; Monday, May 9th, 1803, 299.

[9] Describing the reception of one group of enquirers, Ward writes: "Creeshnoo takes in all these people from time to time. They are entertained for a day or two at our expence [*sic*.], talked with, & then according to their impressions they either go or come forward for baptism" (Ward, Journal MSS, Friday, February 18th, 1803, 282).

the natives against British rule. East India Company officials, their professed Christian faith notwithstanding, were wary lest imprudent dissemination of the gospel offend the religious sentiments of local Hindus and Muslims. On the other hand, the Mission Press served to pacify the Company in that it frequently catered to their printing needs. Fort William College was a frequent and lucrative customer. On one occasion, they ordered a hundred Mahratta dictionaries. On another, they granted the Mission a commission to print a Sanskrit Dictionary. In another order, a request was made for 100 copies of the Indian folk tale collection, *Hitopadesh*, and in yet another case, they received a request for the "publication of books in the Bengali language for use in the classes."[10] In some cases, translation and printing was enjoined *because* British money was offered.[11] An entire thesis could be written on the voluminous publications that rolled forth from the Mission Press and the role of the press in the overall strategy of the Serampore Mission. This essay, however, will consider Ward's role as printer in the larger context of his spirituality in connection with the many other roles he fulfilled at the Mission.

By the time Ward returned from his international tour (1819–1821), Serampore's printing operation demanded his oversight of a massive printing operation, including a foundry for the manufacture of metal types, nineteen presses, and over two hundred people who were employed at the printing office.[12] Indeed, Ward grew so busy with his responsibilities at the press that he wondered if all of the activity were indeed justified with respect to their end goal. "I know not how it would be if conversions among the natives were very numerous, our hands are so full with translating and other foundation work. I am encouraged to hope, that the foundation is not thus laying, to such an extent and to such a depth, without reason."[13] According to Christopher Smith, "As the senior partners produced prodigious publications and multiplied their translation projects, they departed from a 'pilgrim' model of mission."[14] This criticism has some merit, but printer was just one of many roles that Ward played so that his impact as a missionary was not limited solely to it.

Itinerant Preacher & Pastor
Though printing was Ward's vocation, it is noteworthy how seldom it received attention in his *Journal*; instead, the early portions of his *Journal* chronicled the almost ceaseless itinerating that was carried out by missionaries and national brethren alike.[15] The frequency of these entries reveals much concerning the prominence of itinerancy in the Mission's

---

10 Ward, Journal MSS, 437, 364, 220, 81.

11 This was the case with the Chinese translation and publication of the Scriptures which John Marshman championed. Ward offers the following wry description of its genesis: "Bro. Carey has brought word that the College will be at the expence [*sic*], of providing men from Macow who know Chinese & Latin, if any one of our family will begin to learn & superintend a translation of the Scriptures into the Chinese language. Bro. Marshman, I suppose, will embrace the opportunity" (Ward, Journal MSS, Saturday, February 16th, 1805, 409–10).

12 Marshman, *Life and Times*, 1:421, 2:249; Stennett, *Memoirs of the Life of the Rev. William Ward*, 183.

13 Stennett, *Memoirs of the Life of the Rev. William Ward*, 183–4.

14 Smith, *Serampore Enterprise*, 195.

15 Ward had engaged in hamlet preaching while at Ewood Hall. Fuller and Carey both regarded it as indispensable in their missionary effort.

mission strategy as well as Ward's personal beliefs and piety. Though examples abound, the following will suffice as evidence for the same.

> I then told them that three of us were come to this country to make known the true way of salvation. I then attempted to describe the fall, & consequent universal depravity of man. Then the free mercy of God in salvation, & the fruits of faith in Xt's holiness & heaven, I told them that to make this known we were come to India; that we had printed part of God's word in Bengalee.[16]

In this excerpt we see exactly what it was that Ward and his colleagues wanted to communicate when they itinerated. These same themes can be seen in his own descriptions of his preaching. Following an outing with his regular itinerating partner, Felix Carey (1786–1822), Ward stated that the "subjects handled" included the "depravity of man, the inefficacy of the Hindoo religion, the death of Xt., the day of judgment."[17] Once again, after speaking with a European who feared death, Ward summarized that "I went & talked with him, of repentance, faith in Xt. & the grace of God."[18] On another occasion, he stated, "My principle aim was to bring home their sins—to shew that God would judge them either as righteous or unrighteous, not as Hindoos."[19]

Demonstrated here are the grand themes of evangelical Calvinism—the sinful depravity of man, the sufficiency of Christ, and God's free, gracious, and effectual choice of sinners unto salvation. Another example, taken from his *Reflections on the Word of God For Every Day of the Year*, written toward the end of his life, demonstrates these theological emphases were persistent throughout his missionary career.

> The doctrine which our Lord teaches us when he says "Without me ye can do nothing," is, not only that his death is the sole procuring cause of salvation; but that the blessings of this salvation are never applied to the heart but through his efficient agency. There can be no real prayer without a previous sense of want, and without what is called the spirit of prayer: now our Saviour bestows both these or we shall never call on his name. We are not able to repent, but Christ is exalted as a Prince and a Saviour, 'to *give* repentance. Faith is his gift; and all good thoughts and good works are impossible to us but as he renews within us "a right spirit."[20]

Ward's theological convictions concerning man's depravity and God's gracious sovereignty influenced his view of both. In the case of pagan sinners Ward strove to reach, he was moved to pity and compassion. Once, while itinerating with one of the national brethren, a discouraged Prasad remarked concerning their audience in Dinagepore, "The people of these upper parts will never be converted," to which Ward replied: "'Never' is saying too much, but I feel towards them as much pain as I should if I were to see a person

---

16 Ward, Journal MSS, Wednesday, October 28th, 1801, 184.

17 Ward, Journal MSS, Saturday, February 7th, 1801, 139.

18 Ward, Journal MSS, Thursday, October 22nd, 1801, 181.

19 Ward, Journal MSS, Thursday, September 29th, 1803, 327–8.

20 William Ward, *Reflections On the Word of God For Every Day in the Year In Two Volumes* (Serampore: Mission Press, 1822), 1:174.

drowning & on account of the distance of the water I was unable to help him."[21] In the case of the God to whom Ward longed to introduce the Indian masses, Ward was moved to utter dependence on Him for any fruit of eternal significance as seen in the following record of itinerancy in Nadia District which he felt was, "as unfavorable a place for the Gospel as any in Bengal."[22]

> Every conversation that I have with the natives makes me perceive more & more at what a distance these immense multitudes of immortals are from embracing the truth as it is in Jesus. Their prejudices, habits, cast, aversion to English manners & people, & ignorance of the religion of nature & conscience, proves that God only can make them put on the profession of Xt. in sincerity. Yet still the work seems nearer than ever:—who can despair—"God's eternal thought moves on"—& miracles have been performed already.[23]

Humanly speaking, the conversion of the Indian peoples seemed impossible, but Ward's dependence on God bolstered his confidence and prevented despair. Another example of this confidence is seen in the following excerpt written to a friend while on a mission outing in Jessore. "We have tried our weapons and we know their strength; the doctrine of the Cross is stronger than the cast, and in this we shall be *more than conquerors.*"[24] Though the increasing demands of discipleship of new believers, mentorship of younger missionary colleagues, and of responsibilities in the print shop meant less time for itinerating, Ward rued the loss and continued throughout his life to acknowledge its importance in their mission and his fondness for it.[25]

---

21 Ward, Journal MSS, Wednesday, November 23rd, 1803, 348.

22 Ward, Journal MSS, Wednesday, September 28th, 1803, 326.

23 Ward, Journal MSS, Wednesday, September 28th, 1803, 327.

24 Stennett, *Memoirs of the Life of the Rev. William Ward*, 144.

25 As early as 1802, Ward and his evangelism partner, Felix Carey, were beginning to spend less time in itinerancy and more time in discipleship of new believers (Ward, Journal MSS, Lord's Day, May 9th, 1802, 230). Stennett, speaking of same phenomenon around the year 1808, assigns the reason for decline in itinerancy to, "the progress of the translations and the increasing number of them," and to the increasing need of oversight of more recent missionary arrivals from England and the increasing number of native preachers (Stennett, *Memoirs of the Life of the Rev. William Ward*, 160–61). Alongside these activities, there was an uptick in fruit among Asiatics (those of mixed European and Indian ancestry) and Europeans. Ward welcomed these "advancements" but at the same time recognized that, "Our success among the natives is slackened, owing, I suppose, in some measure to our not being able to itinerate" (Stennett, *Memoirs of the Life of the Rev. William Ward*, 164). Again, in an entry on the Lord's Day, April 14th, 1811, Ward expresses being uneasy that, "for some time we have not been able to do no more in the itinerating line in this neighbourhood" (Ward, Journal MSS, Lord's Day, April 14th, 1811, 752). But in the midst of the increasing demands on his time, the fondness for itinerancy and evangelism remained. In the midst of government strictures on preaching in Calcutta, Ward remarked, "Oh! if [sic.] we could get leave to itinerate ourselves, & fix stations in different parts, we should care for nothing else in the world" (Ward, Journal MSS, Saturday, August 30th, 1806, 505). While itinerating in Dinagepore, "Perhaps in all these labours we are casting bread on the waters, which will not be seen till after many days,, but I never felt myself more in the path of duty" (Ward, Journal MSS, Wednesday, October 5th, 1803, 332). Even in the year prior to his international tour of England, Holland, and America, Ward waxed lyrical in an 1818 letter to a friend as he described his ideal retirement: "I have been thinking of looking out for some spot for my future retirement, where I may erect a bungalow and have a Christian village, and devote my remaining days to the instruction of inquirers and the formation of young Hindoos for the ministry. It must be by the side of one of these lakes. I do not know what destiny may await me, but at present I do contemplate something of this kind, if I can but see a comfortable settlement of things at Serampore, and I see nothing now so desirable as such a mode of closing life" (Marshman, *Life And Times*, 2:161). In noting the decline in itinerancy, Serampore scholar, A. Christopher Smith finds fault with

In addition to serving as itinerant preacher and evangelist, Ward also served faithfully as pastor, both at the Mission Church and at the church in Calcutta which in time became Lal Bazaar Chapel and today is known as Carey Baptist Church.[26] In addition to these, he regularly filled the pulpit at various worship services that took place in the homes of dissenters in the city at a time when they were not allowed to hold public worship.[27] Though the Trio acknowledged their ineffectiveness in preaching for conversion among native Hindus and Muslims, Ward's and others' efforts were greatly blessed among Asiatics (those of mixed Indian and Portuguese background) and British soldiers.[28] As a result, many traced the beginning of their serious impressions to a sermon they heard from Ward.[29] Ward's labor in his pastoral work was indefatigable, often preaching in English and Bangla three or more times on a Lord's Day, visiting prisoners in jail and the infirm in the hospital, distributing Bibles and tracts, and all in the tropical heat of a Calcutta without electric fans in which he once quipped, "Preaching in black clothes in this climate is a sad burden. My clothes have been three times as wet as dung today, & the very papers in my pockets have been dyed black with sweat."[30]

---

the Trio stating, "Although the foundational *Form of Agreement* forcefully asserted that open-air evangelism was each missionary's primary duty, the troika rarely ever engaged in such work after 1805" (Smith, *Serampore Enterprise*, 313). Smith is right to recognize of a disparity between the principles of the *SFA* and reality at the Mission in the area of itinerancy, but he fails to give credence to the Trio's own admissions of their inability in itinerancy when compared to the skill of the national workers. As early as 1801, Ward observed, "There has been but little new in our Bengallee Services lately, except that the people manifest mostly a very great contempt of the word. We can seldom raise half a score people at once. Yet at Creeshnoo's house a score three, four & half a dozen people hear daily, & get papers" (Ward, Journal MSS, Lord's Day, April 19th, 1801, 151). Ward expressed doubt that Europeans would ever be used to, "convert souls by preaching, in this country" (Ward, Journal MSS, Monday, November 13 [15], 1802, 268). Even the pamphlets which were printed by Ward were better received at the hands of Creeshnoo than Ward himself. "At length I offered them books. Nobody would receive them. We were going, but Creeshnoo being a little behind, they eagerly took them of[f] him, so that in a little time we had scarcely one left with us" (Ward, Journal MSS, Tuesday, October 13th, 1801, 175). And again, "Almost all our Members lately have been brought forward in their first impressions thro' Creeshnoo & his family" (Ward, Journal MSS, Monday, May 9th, 1803, 299). When these admissions of the superior usefulness of national workers over European ones is duly considered, a picture emerges of a Trio that remained convicted of the need for itinerancy and felt strong affection for the same, but who, over time, gravitated to those pursuits for which they were most gifted.

26 Ward was named co-pastor along with Marshman and Carey at the Serampore church on October 5th, 1805 (Ward, Journal MSS, October 5, 1805, 440). Carey, Marshman, and Ward later served as co-pastors at Lal Bazaar Chapel from the time of its opening on January 1, 1809, "until 16th June 1825, when the Survivors of them, the Revd. Dr. Carey and Marshman resigned the Pastorate publicly on the ordination of the Revd. W. Robinson," who served from that day until November the 11th, 1838 (*Lal Bazar Baptist Church, Calcutta Letter-Book & Records With _____y, December 1876 to April 1885*, 443; located at Carey Baptist Church, Kolkata). In addition to the co-pastorate of the Trio, they were joined by Missionaries John Lawson (1887–1825) and Eustace Carey (1791–1855) from September, 1815. See *Periodical Account* 6:91–92; Edward Steane Wenger, ed., *The Story of the Lall Bazar Baptist Church Calcutta. Being The History Of Carey's Church From 24th April 1800 To The Present Day* (Calcutta: Edinburgh Press, 1908), 86. Both Eustace Carey and John Lawson resigned from the pastorate of Lal Bazaar Chapel in October 1819 (Wenger, ed., *Story of the Lall Bazar Baptist Church Calcutta*, 145).

27 Some of the hosts of these "house churches" include Mr. Rolt, Mr. Lindeman, Mr. Derozio, and Mr. Petruse, the Armenian.

28 Eighty-seven soldiers from various regiments were received as members by baptism at Lal Bazaar Chapel from 1810 to 1815, see Wenger, ed., *Story of the Lall Bazar Baptist Church Calcutta*, 61.

29 For instance, an Ananda "dated the change that had taken place in her heart and conduct from a sermon which I preached at the Bengalee school one Lord's Day morning" (Ward, Journal MSS, Saturday, November 2, 1805, 448). A Mr. Burford became anxious over his soul after hearing Ward preach (Ward, Monday, January 27, 1806, 473).

30 Ward, Journal MSS, Lord's Day, June 17, 1810, 729.

Nevertheless, we are concerned with Ward's heart in these pastoral endeavors, and we see it on full display as he gave pastoral advice to his Ewood Hall fellow and eventual memoirist, Samuel Stennett. The following quote reveals both Ward's evangelical Calvinistic warmness and the connection between Ward's preaching and his peacemaking:

> Keep this constantly in mind. You may preach twice a week, and have a great name among certain kinds of Christians for orthodoxy or oratory; but you are a minister of the gospel so far exactly, as your zeal, your gifts, your efforts and your conduct, are calculated to produce the conversion of souls. For my part, I set a very small value upon most modern doctrinal sermons and controversial writings; and I think their value will be less appreciated, when Christians *see as they are seen*. I would not discard controversy altogether; but I dislike the devil (as the Hindoos would say) in its belly; and I fear very few controversial writers could say, while they were writing, *not I, but Christ that liveth in me*. I would not discard doctrinal sermons; but I confess I have seen or heard few, that had either a devotional or a practical tendency; and that, in which there is neither devotion nor practice, is rather worse than nothing ... Study—yes, study to be quiet—but above all, study to get at the affections, the consciences, and the false refuges of sinners:—study to be useful—then you will become a spiritual father ... If you become a useful, [*sic*.] you will first be (as the Puritans said) a painful preacher of the gospel.[31]

Over the course of his career, Ward did not hold himself aloof to controversy when it was warranted.[32] But as seen above, neither was he fond of it. He was irenic, not polemical. He was not averse to doctrine, but he bemoaned showy dry doctrine that obfuscated heartwarming gospel truths. Ward loved doctrine that was "useful" to transform men's lives and increase their love for Christ. His gospel presentations, sermons, and devotional writings are full of doctrine of a robust evangelical Calvinist stamp. He and the rest of the missionaries considered these doctrines of sovereign grace, "glorious."[33]

Mentor
Another role Ward relished was that of mentor and father figure to many in the Serampore Mission. This included the children of fellow missionaries and junior missionary colleagues, for whom Ward, "acted *in loco parentis* as a much-appreciated 'uncle.'"[34] In addition, Ward took great interest in the spiritual and ministerial development of the Bengali evangelists and pastors with whom he labored. As the following quotes make clear, the spiritual progress of neither group was a given. But Ward's steady, intentional, and godly influence was a welcome ballast during the stormy times of youth and frequent backslidings of new converts.

---

31 Ward to Stennett, May, 1803. Stennett, *Memoirs of the Life of the Rev. William Ward*, 118–22.

32 For example, Ward willingly entered conflict with the British government during the Persian Pamphlet controversy of 1807 (J.C. Marshman, *Life and Times*, 307ff) and with the Baptist Missionary Society when their independence in the Serampore Mission was at stake (see Ward's letter to Society in J.C. Marshman, *Life and Times*, 209ff).

33 *Periodical Accounts Relative to the Baptist Missionary Society. Baptist Missionary Society Archives, 1792–1914. (London, England)* (Nashville, TN: Historical Commission, Southern Baptist Convention, 1981), 3:198.

34 Smith, *Serampore Enterprise*, 31.

Though he bore many responsibilities in the Mission, "Mr. Ward ... interested himself much in the prosperity of the family, particularly of the younger branches of it."[35] The following excerpt reveals the manner in which this interest was expressed:

> I have begun a meeting in my room, in which Felix, William, John Fernandez & I engage in prayer in Bengallee, & bring a piece written in this language of our own composition not less than ten lines ... We pray that we may be Missionaries; & that the heathen may be saved. We meet once a week, at 6 in the morning.[36]

He describes a similar meeting six years later: "I was at the Bengalee School in the morning; had John [Marshman] and Jonathan [Carey] & Francis & Jonathan Hasted in my room to talk to them, after dinner."[37] And again in 1810, on the eve of the Mission's anniversary, after spending time with the rest, "I had the young people of the family separately, in my room to talk with them.--I found them all more or less affected with what I said."[38]

A similar *modus operandi* is seen in his discipleship of the native brethren. On Monday, August 17th, 1801, Ward recorded, "I have Creeshnoo & Gokal's children to catechize every Monday evening."[39] Ward's investment in the spiritual development of Bengalis was still the same eight years later.

> In getting accounts of their experience I have been several times pleased lately. On a Lord's-Day evening, at some one of their houses; I generally enquire, when it falls to my lot to be at home & amongst them at these times, how things are respecting the power of the truth on their hearts; & I try to deal as close as I can with the unbaptized. These meetings I have often found very pleasant.[40]

These represent intentional efforts Ward made to mentor expat and native youngsters alike. But the same pastoral heart is seen in more spontaneous efforts that were expended along the way. On one occasion, he enforced that "the necessity of private prayer on Creeshnoo" and inquired whether he asked a blessing on his food. Creeshnoo replied that he had done so ever since receiving Christ and went on to describe the way he prayed with his family every morning and evening and instructed them on the Sabbath.[41] Later that year Ward related a conversation that proceeded from an impromptu visit from a national brother named Gokal.

> Gokal came into my room one evening & asked, whether it was right that he should always have his mind on Xt.';s [*sic.*] death. He said by always keeping his thoughts on that, his mind got dry & exhausted. This is a very common thing amongst Hindoos to

---

35 Stennett, Stennett, *Memoirs of the Life of the Rev. William Ward*, 162.

36 Ward, Journal MSS, Lord's Day, May 17th, 1801, 153.

37 Ward, Journal MSS, Lord's Day, July 5th, 1807, 556.

38 Ward, Journal MSS, Lord's Day, January 7th, 1810, 719.

39 Ward, Journal MSS, Monday, August 17th, 1801, 167.

40 Ward, Journal MSS, Monday, December 4th, 1809, 710.

41 Ward, Journal MSS, Friday, February 13th, 1801, 139.

think that holiness consists in always thinking of one thing, or one name; & if a name, to be always repeating it. I told him that we were to act by divine things as we did by natural ones, think of all & learn all, tho' some were of prime importance. If ever he thought his mind dry or exhausted the Holy Spirit was to be his life.[42]

Ward's role as mentor was not an "official" role but one he took on himself, arising more from affection than from duty. This is seen especially in his response when those under his charge were either not progressing in the faith or falling into sin. Regarding the latter, the children of the other members of the Trio were most notorious. In Ward's *Journal* entry for Friday, August 12th, 1803, he wrote: "Tuesday night to our great grief Wm. Carey [Jnr.] was caught by a maid-servant trying to get into the young lady's sleeping room. It was in the middle of the night."[43] The "young lady" in question was a "Miss Herklots, a child of 10 years old," whom young William had been trying to court contrary to "repeated advice" and "a solemn promise made to Mr. Marshman, & to the rules of the family."[44] Following this shameful event, Ward and Joshua Marshman "had a long conversation with Wm. (Carey Jnr.) in which we tried to make him sensible of the dreadful nature of falsehood, & of the scandal brought upon the cause by his attempt to get into the young ladies [*sic*.] room in the middle of the night. He made not the least reply."[45]

Similarly, on May 2, 1806, Ward records a similar scandal with more dire consequences: "This evening we held our church meeting, when Mohun & Roop were restored to fellowship, & John [Marshman] was excluded for cohabiting with an unmarried woman."[46] In Ward's original handwritten journal, the man who received church discipline for cohabiting with an unmarried woman was merely, "John." When transcribing Ward's journal, Daniel Potts inserted "Marshman" here. However, Peter de Vries pointed out that Potts' assertion was mistaken, as de Vries noted that if the culprit were John Clark Marshman, he would have been a bit shy of his twelfth birthday at this time. It is more likely that the "John" in question was a so-called Portuguese man of Muslim background, who "received impressions under Bro. Carey at Calcutta" and was subsequently received into the church at Serampore and baptized three years before this event.[47]

Ward was greatly disheartened to see such indifference and brazenness despite the care he had taken in their religious instruction. In another journal entry, he wrote: "In the

---

42 Ward, Journal MSS, Lord's Day, August 30th, 1801, 169.

43 Ward, Journal MSS, August 12th, 1803, 318.

44 Ward, Journal MSS, August 12th, 1803, 318.

45 Ward, Journal MSS, Thursday, August 25th, 1803, 319.

46 Ward, Journal MSS, Friday, May 2, 1806, 486.

47 Ward, Journal MSS, Lord's Day, July 3, 1803, 311. The manner in which de Vries discovered John's true identity is fascinating, as he stated that "On our mysterious (sad case of) John, I checked Wenger's notes 'Register of members admitted to the Serampore--Lall Bazar Church,' and found one 'John' [without last name] who was baptized on 3rd July 1803, and 'excluded for immorality on 30th May 1806'. Source: Edward S. Wenger, *Missionary Biographies*, Vol IV, p 261, mss ... I checked Wenger's *Story of Lall-Bazar Baptist Church*, and he appears there as 'John' on p. xx of the Appendix. All the other John's have last names, and have separate entries: John Thomas, John Fountain, John Chamberlain, John Lewis Fernandez, and John Biss. The baptismal date solves the problem, however; Checking the *PA*, Xiii (1804), 409, Marshman's Journal entry for July 3rd 1803, I found a 'John, a Portuguese from Calcutta was also baptized' ... So the issue can now easily be resolved" (Peter de Vries, e-mail message to author, December 27, 2018).

afternoon I talked to John Marshman with many tears. Jabez [Carey], Jonathan [Carey] & John are growing up to manhood fast: no signs of real grace. Many many prayers are offered up for these children. Jabez the eldest seems far from righteousness."[48] A year later, it was the same: "Besides preaching, I had the bigger boys of the school, one by one, up into my study after dinner, & talked with them. They hear, & promise, but their goodness is like the morning dew. Jabez [Carey], Jonathan [Carey] & John Marshman are still in the gall of bittering. The first is the most hopeless."[49]

Even more incidents are recorded in Ward's journal regarding the backslidings of their national brethren. Frequently they were found making visits to the houses of "bad women," stealing, or returning to their former faith, whether Hindu or Muslim. These events grieved Ward greatly and, but for his faith in Christ and his gospel, he would have despaired and given up.[50] Ward's investment in these new believers, his longing for their spiritual advancement, and grief when they did not, are all evidence of his heart for the sanctification and progress in the faith of junior missionaries and national converts alike.

Ward was more encouraged with the development of Carey's oldest surviving son, Felix. At once, Ward noted that he spent the entire night in religious exercises.[51] Felix was Ward's partner in itinerancy when he was a mere 15 years of age.[52] A month later, Ward wrote in a letter that "God, I hope, has blessed my labours to the conversion of Mr. Carey's too (*sic*.) eldest sons."[53] Ward not only mentored Felix in the faith but also in the printing office, and in the period between John Fountain's and Daniel Brunsdon's (1777–1801) deaths, he encouraged himself with the thought that "if I die, Felix Carey will be able to print."[54] When it came to Felix's ordination at the age of 21, it was Ward who gave him his charge, recording that he was, "a good deal affected, & I wished to feel thankful."[55] Felix would go on to nobly represent the Serampore Mission in pioneering work in Burma. As Felix was laying a foundation there, Ward notes his desire to set up a press in Burma, which Ward admitted, "He knows well how to conduct, as he labored diligently many years in the printing-office at Serampore."[56]

It is also significant to consider Ward's use of a children's catechism in mentorship. On Saturday, June 6th, 1801, Ward read to his brethren a catechism that he had written for the children of converted natives, which he hoped to translate with Felix's help.[57] This they did and in his catechism of Bengali children, he invested in them much as he had in the

48 Ward, Journal MSS, Lord's Day, December 24th, 1809, 716.

49 Ward, Journal MSS, Lord's Day, July 22nd, 1810, 731.

50 Ward, Journal MSS, Monday, November 1st, 1802, 265.

51 Ward, Journal MSS, Monday, October 20th, 1800, 108.

52 Ward, Journal MSS, Thursday, October 28th, 1800, 109.

53 Stennett, *Memoirs of the Life of the Rev. William Ward*, 104.

54 Ward, Journal MSS, Saturday, March 14th, 1801, 145 and in a letter to a friend, March 24th, 1801 (Stennett, *Memoirs of the Life of the Rev. William Ward*, 94).

55 Ward, Journal MSS, Lord's Day, August 23rd, 1807, 575.

56 *Monthly Circular Letters Relative to the Missions in India, Established by a Society in England, Called the "Baptist Missionary Society,"* 6 (1813): 11.

57 Ward, Journal MSS, Saturday, June 6th, 1801, 157; Ward, Journal MSS, Lord's Day, July 12th, 1801, 164.

missionary children and native brethren. "We do this in turn on a Lord's day afternoon, & go over the sermon, requiring from them the text, & what they remember of it."[58] A Bengali version of Isaac Watts' (1674–1748) children's catechism was also used, of which some of the younger catechumens were able to repeat by heart, 160 lines.[59] With the adult national believers, there is a note after a baptism, "These people are under daily instruction," and two years later Ward records that, "We have begun to go thro' the Testament daily with our native brethren. Each one reads a verse & tries to give the meaning, & one of us helps them out."[60]

In time, this bore fruit as one convert, Komol, began a catechetical school himself, using the same work.[61] As was the content of Ward's preaching, so, "Creeshnoo's chief topic in his daily conversations with the natives was, "the love & death of Xt. & the fruits of faith."[62] Similarly, as the Serampore family met regularly for prayer, so Ward records a prayer meeting begun by the natives. Ward was a mentor and pastor by heart and nature. He invested in others from the overflow of his own spirituality. The fruit of that investment is seen in these junior missionaries and native brethren above who cherished the same gracious doctrines and preached the same gospel that Ward did.

Author/Draftsman
Ward's years as editor of the *Derby Mercury*, and *Hull Advertiser* rendered him uniquely qualified both to draft works on behalf of the Trio and Mission and to author works of his own. The impetus for Ward's own works came from within, while much of what he drafted he received—sometimes ruefully—from Carey or Marshman. In 1805, it was recorded that the Mission Press had completed a small volume called *Happy Deaths* (now lost), being a compilation from evangelical magazines of the time, containing "accounts of the happy deaths of young people." Ward continues wryly, "I hope it may be useful here, & perhaps in England. Bro. Carey, Marshman & I have signed a Recommendatory Address prefixed. This address, & the drudgery of compilation, fell on me."[63] In 1801, upon Anglican chaplain Claudius Buchanan's (1766–1815) recommendation and Carey's request, Ward drew up a proposal for a chapel in Calcutta, whose funds and preachers would be supplied by different dissenting denominations.[64] In 1805, Ward drafted the principles by which the Mission would be run in the landmark *Serampore Form of Agreement*.[65] In December of 1809, on the tenth anniversary of the Mission's establishment in Serampore, Ward drew up "a general review of the progress which had been made during this period … at the

---

58 Ward, Journal MSS, Lord's Day, March 28th, 1802, 221.

59 Ward, Journal MSS, Monday, June 28th, 1802, 240.

60 Ward, Journal MSS, Tuesday, June 1st, 1802, 235; Lord's Day, April 15th, 1804, 370.

61 Ward, Journal MSS, Friday, May 22nd, 1802, 229.

62 Ward, Journal MSS, Friday, June 12th, 1801, 158; Ward, Journal MSS, Thursday, January 12th, 1802, 203.

63 Ward, Journal MSS, Thursday, September 12th, 1805, 436.

64 Ward, Journal MSS, Friday, September 4th, 1801, 169. This chapel later became Lal Bazaar Chapel and is called Carey Baptist Church today.

65 The *SFA* drafted by Ward was "explicitly stated by John Clark Marshman" in his *Life and Times*, 1.229, and was "confirmed by internal evidence and questions of style" ("The Serampore Form of Agreement," *Baptist Quarterly* 12.5 [1947]: 125).

request of his brethren."⁶⁶ In the midst of wranglings with the BMS over ownership of Serampore Mission property in 1816, after long and anxious deliberation, it was Ward who drew up a "comfortable settlement," which was then submitted to his colleagues and then sent, in a private letter to a friend on the BMS committee in England.⁶⁷ It was Ward that maintained the Mission's journal, which ran from he and his colleagues' embarkation for India in 1799 until October, 1811, when it was superseded by the *Circular Letters*.⁶⁸ So, the Mission often turned to Ward when it came time to pen their thoughts. It is significant to pay some attention to Ward's authorship of the *Serampore Form of Agreement*, as it is one of his most enduring missiological contributions as well as providing great insight into his personal piety.

The forerunner of the *SFA* was a set of rules that the Baptist Mission adopted in early 1800 "for the government of the family."⁶⁹ In general terms, it stipulated that "All are equal, all preach & pray in turn, one superintends the family for a month & then another; Bro. C[arey] is treasurer & has the regulation of the Medicine Chest; Brother Fountain is his librarian. The Saturday evening is devoted to the adjusting of differences, & pledging ourselves to love each other."⁷⁰ These rules appear to have been sufficient during the Mission's infancy, but with the arrival of five new missionaries by the end of 1804, there was a need to formalize Mission guidelines for posterity.⁷¹ As a result, Ward wrote in his *Journal* on Saturday, October 5th, 1805: "At our evening council I delivered to each Bren. A copy of a 'Form of Agreement respecting the Principles upon which we think it our duty to act in instructing the Heathen.' I wished much that we should leave to our successors something like this, & therefore drew it up, read it to the Brethren, & to-night gave to each a copy for their corrections & additions."⁷² The following day, the Mission celebrated the twelfth anniversary of the Baptist Missionary Society with prayer, multiple preachings, baptisms, and the reorganization of the church at Serampore by installing missionaries Mardon, Biss, Moore, and Rowe and two Indian converts, Krishna Pal (1764–1822) and

---

66 Marshman, *Life and Times*, 1:421.

67 Marshman, *Life and Times*, 2:137. Though this letter was sent privately until the time a more mature plan could be sent to the Society, it was submitted publicly at the annual meeting of the Society in October 1816. The misunderstanding that ensued has become known as the Serampore Controversy and was not completely resolved when the latest surviving member of the Trio, Joshua Marshman, died in 1837.

68 Ward began printing monthly *Circular Letters* from December 1807. As he later explained to Society member, John Sutcliffe (1752–1814), he made this move as the letters "provided a means of getting more material to England on the progress of the mission than could ever be done through his journal and private correspondence" (E. Daniel Potts, "William Ward's Missionary Journal," *Baptist Quarterly* 25.3 [1973]: 113). On the same page of this article, Potts cites a letter from Ward to Fuller in 1811, in which Ward acknowledged that the *Circular Letters* he had begun left little time for the Journal. While Ward may considered the *Circular Letters* superior to the Journal for relating material from the Mission, it reads as a compilation of letters devoid of the unedited commentary and wry comments found Ward's Journal.

69 Ward, Journal MSS, Saturday, January 18th, 1800, 66.

70 Ward, Journal MSS, Saturday, January 18th, 1800, 66.

71 John Chamberlain (1777–1821) arrived in Serampore in 1802, while John Biss (1776–1807), William Moore (1776–1844), Joshua Rowe (1781–1823), and Richard Mardon (1775–1812) arrived in 1804.

72 Ward, Journal MSS, Saturday, October 5th, 1805, 440.

Krishna Prasad as deacons and Marshman and Ward as co-pastors with Carey.[73]

The agreement is divided into a preamble, ten sections, and an epilogue, stating the principles which governed the Mission. Section one explained the absolute necessity of setting an "infinite value upon immortal souls."[74] Section two explained the importance of gaining knowledge of cultural and religious "snares and delusions" in which the Indian heathen were held.[75] Section three described the need to abstain from "those things which would increase their prejudices against the gospel" and to humbly pursue the example of the apostle Paul who became all things to all men that some might be saved.[76] Section four talked about the urgency of taking advantage of every opportunity to communicate the gospel to the natives.[77] Section five explained the expediency of making "the great subject of our preaching, Christ the crucified."[78] Section six explained the necessity of kind and equitable treatment of the natives that they might have "entire confidence in us."[79] Section seven described the importance of discipling native converts in "the great principles of the gospel."[80] Section eight is about the duty of building up their native brothers and sisters that the gospel might, by their hands, be permanently established in India.[81] Section nine described the need to translate and distribute the "sacred scriptures in the languages of Hindoostan" and to found native "free schools" which they considered important for "future conquests of the gospel."[82] Section ten described the fitness of prayer in their labor, which they held to lie, "at the root of all personal godliness."[83] The epilogue described the imperative of denying themselves for the sake of the gospel of Christ and its progress among the Indian peoples, with special reference to common ownership of property within the Mission.[84]

Nevertheless, the conviction underlying all ten principles is stated in the Agreement's preamble:

> We are firmly persuaded that Paul might plant and Appollos [*sic*.] water in vain in any part of the world, did not God give the increase. We are sure, that only those who are ordained to eternal life will believe, and that God alone can add to the church such as shall be saved. Nevertheless we cannot but observe with admiration, that Paul, the

---

73 "The Serampore Form of Agreement," *Baptist Quarterly* 12.5 (1947): 126. In the citation above and in J.C. Marshman's *Life and Times*, the SFA's writing is attributed to Ward (Marshman, *Life and Times*, 1:229). The agreement can be found in the *Periodical Accounts*, 3:198–211.

74 *PA*, 3:199.

75 *PA*, 3:200.

76 *PA*, 3:200.

77 *PA*, 3:201.

78 *PA*, 3:201.

79 *PA*, 3:202.

80 *PA*, 3:203.

81 *PA*, 3:205–8.

82 *PA*, 3:208–9.

83 *PA*, 3:210.

84 *PA*, 3:210–1.

great champion for the glorious doctrines of free and sovereign grace, was the most conspicuous for his personal zeal in the work of persuading men to be reconciled to God. In this respect he is a noble example for our imitation."[85]

Like Ward's itinerant preaching, the *SFA*'s preamble also displayed a robust evangelical Calvinism. As the editor of the *Baptist Quarterly* maintained, the *SFA* "has rightly come to be regarded as one of the foundation documents for a study of the missionary strategy of the early nineteenth century. It has, however, more than an historic interest. It remains a moving and challenging statement of the main principles which must underlie the Christian mission in any age and any land."[86] Despite Christopher Smith's numerous criticisms of the *SFA*, he still acknowledges it to be a "milestone."[87]

Husband & Father
Sadly, the wives and families of the Serampore Mission are rarely mentioned in Ward's *Journal* or in the seminal account of the Serampore Mission, J.C. Marshman's *Life and Times*. Nevertheless from scattered information Ward recorded in his *Journal* and personal letters preserved by Samuel Stennett, it is apparent that he loved both his wife and children and cared greatly for their spiritual state. Ward came to the mission field single but on May 10th, 1802, he married Mary Tidd, widow of his deceased missionary colleague John Fountain.[88] According to Ward, "the marriage covenant & ceremony were of my choosing," while it was performed by Carey in the presence of friends, expat and Bengali.[89] Amidst Ward's modest description of the marriage ceremony is a summary of Carey's address which explains much concerning the scant presence in his *Journal* of

---

85 *PA*, 3:198.

86 "The Serampore Form of Agreement," 125.

87 Smith, *Serampore Enterprise*, 39. Smith's critique of the *SFA* can be found in Appendix 3 of *The Serampore Mission Enterprise*, 297–318. In short, he faults the Serampore Mission in general and the Trio in particular for not adhering to the "great principles" of the *SFA*. Specifically, he alleges nonadherence to the principles of Mission economy (common property, from the *SFA* Epilogue), itinerancy, the principles for which are found in Sections I and V of the *SFA*. He finds further fault with the Serampore Mission for failing to apprise the Society in England of revisions in missionary strategy following the 1805 Agreement. Though this is not the place to respond in full to Smith's critique, two general responses will be given. First, Smith excellently pointed out the chronicling changes in Mission strategy through the years, and he is right to note that the *SFA* was not consistently followed as strategy. He also noticed the difference between the "prospective and descriptive" principles set forth in the *SFA* contrasted with the explicit strategy set forth in the *Plan for Taking All Asia* that was drafted by Joshua Marshman in 1806 (See Smith, *Serampore Enterprise*, 305n14). However, in the critique that follows, Smith seems to forget his own distinction, holding the Trio liable for not following a *strategy* in line with the *SFA*. On the contrary, this author would argue that despite changes in strategy, Ward continued to be animated by these great principles.

88 John Fountain was the second missionary sent out by the BMS, arriving in India toward the close of 1796. He came to Bengal on an East India Company ship rated as a servant and subsequently obtained permission from George Udny--an evangelical indigo planter and later succeeded Charles Grant as Commercial Resident at Malda--and David Brown (1763-1812; Anglican chaplain at Ft. William) to journey toward Udny's indigo plantation in Mudnabatty where he joined Carey. Passionate and indiscreet in the expression of his political convictions, he was rebuked numerous times by Andrew Fuller who had already advised noninterference in political matters. He died on August 20, 1800, before his first wedding anniversary while Mary was pregnant with their first child. See Marshman, *Life And Times*, 1:75–77; A. Christopher Smith, "William Ward, Radical Reform, and Missions in the 1790s," *American Baptist Quarterly*, 10 (1991): 239; Ward, Journal MSS, Monday, August 18th, 1800–Friday, August 29th, 1800, 94–95; Stennett, *Memoirs of the Life of the Rev. William Ward*, 108–9; Smith, *Serampore Enterprise*, 31.

89 Ward, Journal MSS, Monday, May 10th, 1802, 230.

details concerning his wife and marriage: "Then Bro. C. made a very appropriate address to the married couple on the duties of husband & wife, & made a very pleasant allusion to our family situation, in which all personal interests were swallowed up in the interest of the whole."[90]

The "family situation," to which Carey alludes, is not the situation of the new family created by the wedding but rather the common-property situation of the Serampore family. In this arrangement, personal possessions, excepting a small allowance for each member, were held in common. But, in addition to this, it was a general principle that interests of the Mission come before personal and familial interests. To some degree, it would seem even Ward's marriage to a deceased colleague's widow was an outworking of this principle. Perhaps there is a hint of an arranged marriage for the sake of the family in Ward's comment that "this marriage had been intended for some time, but circumstances hindered."[91] With a brief comment following his marriage, it seems William and Mary Ward were happy together. Ward wrote, "We are very happy in our family, enjoying uninterrupted harmony & love; our temporal wants are all supplied."[92] Furthermore, from a couple of comments during Mrs. Ward's illnesses, it is evident Ward cared greatly for her. In March or 1805, Ward "sat for two or three hours near in a violent state of distraction," when he feared his wife would miscarry their child.[93] On another occasion, he writes, "I took down Mrs. Ward to Dr. Hare, respecting a pain in her side. He … removed a mountain of fears from me, by declaring that the pain in her side was not an affection [infection] of the liver; but is only arose [sic.] from cold."[94] He also had regard for her need of rest and renewal as seen in the frequent recording of Mrs. Ward's "annual trip" to Calcutta.[95] In a comment perhaps demeaning to a wife's domestic duties, he nonetheless displays a keen desire for the spiritual development of all the wives of the mission. On the occasion of Hannah Marshman's beginning of experience meetings for native sisters, he records his approbation adding, "I cannot bear that our sisters should be mere house-wives."[96]

Ward was father to five children including Mary's son by her late husband, John Fountain, who died shortly before the boy's birth.[97] In addition to this adopted son, Ward and Mary had four daughters, two dying young, and two surviving to adulthood.[98]

---

90 Ward, Journal MSS, Monday, May 10th, 1802, 231.

91 Ward, Journal MSS, Monday, May 10th, 1802, 230.

92 Ward, Journal MSS, Monday, November 13th [15th], 1802, 268.

93 Ward, Journal MSS, Friday, March 22nd, 1805, 413.

94 Ward, Journal MSS, Saturday, February 11th, 1809, 687.

95 Ward, Journal MSS, 529, 616–7, 682, 702, 744.

96 Ward, Journal MSS, Tuesday, May 25th [26th], 1807, 550.

97 Stennett, Stennett, *Memoirs of the Life of the Rev. William Ward*, 108–9; Smith, *Serampore Enterprise*, 31.

98 Stennett, Stennett, *Memoirs of the Life of the Rev. William Ward*, 112; Smith, *Serampore Enterprise*, 31. William and Mary's first daughter was Hannah, born around August 1803 (Stennett, Stennett, *Memoirs of the Life of the Rev. William Ward*, 135). Their second, Mary, was born in 1806 and died of a sore throat in 1812, the same year as numerous other Mission family deaths and the devastating fire that consumed many Scripture translations and other manuscripts (Ward, *Diary of William Ward*, Wednesday, September 14th, 1808, 673; Stennett, Stennett, *Memoirs of the Life of the Rev. William Ward*, 172, 175–6, 178; *Circular Letters*, 6:3) Another daughter was born in 1808, but whether Ann or Amelia is unclear. Ann is mentioned in a letter

His love for his children and concern for their spiritual state is evident in the following correspondence to a friend on March 26, 1812, following both the devastating fire that destroyed most of the printing office and the death of their second daughter, Mary.

> Notwithstanding this loss by the fire so great, I felt much more for the loss of my dear child, than for this; she was a charming child, and had entwined herself round my heart so much, that I seem never to have seen affliction till this child was taken from me. I had never calculated on the death of any of my family; but had always been thinking of being taken from them ... I have now two daughters left, and Mrs. Ward's son by Mr. Fountain ... I have many comforts left, and am very happy in my family; but I much wish to see the work of grace begun in the hearts of my children, before I go hence.[99]

Friend & Counselor

For William Ward, friendship is precious, as he wrote in a poem:

> Hail Friendship! Queen of earthly joys,
> Without thee, diadems are toys
> And vain is nature's store,
> With thee I would for ever rest,
> Made by thy smile supremely blest;
> Nor ask the world for more.[100]

Thus, Ward's life is marked by friendship. As Ward wrote about his situation in Calcutta: "I have many friends in this country, whose affection is one of the great consolations in my life. When I go to Calcutta, I could spend a whole week in going from house to house, and in every house I find my friends all eager to make me a guest."[101] Moreover, many looked to him for spiritual counsel, specifically, his colleagues looked to him for counsel in missionary matters.[102] So much was this the case that Joshua Marshman, upon Ward's death, confessed that "I feel the loss of Mr. Ward as a counsellor beyond everything. I never did

---

to a friend "about the beginning of the year 1813" (Stennett, Stennett, *Memoirs of the Life of the Rev. William Ward*, 179). In a letter from 1814, mention is made of Amelia losing sight in one eye due to a neglected cold (Stennett, Stennett, *Memoirs of the Life of the Rev. William Ward*, 187–8).

99 Stennett, Stennett, *Memoirs of the Life of the Rev. William Ward*, 176–7.

100 From "Ode To Friendship," written by Ward in Hull on July 10th, 1797, in Stennett, *Memoirs of the Life of the Rev. William Ward*, 282–3.

101 From a letter dated January 11, 1810, in Stennett, *Memoirs of the Life of the Rev. William Ward*, 166–7.

102 In addition to those mentioned previously who received their first serious impressions from Ward's sermons a Mr. Barlow wrote to Ward expressing concern for his soul and his desire to meet to discuss the same (Ward, Journal MSS, Tuesday, June 23, 1807, 554). Another, one Foster, whom Ward visited in the jail, when read his death sentence, exclaimed, "O that I could see Mr. Ward now!" (Ward, Journal MSS, Friday, December 8, 1809, 711).

After going through a split with fellow BMS colleague, John Chamblerain, the Trio was trying to decide where William Robinson (1784–1853) should be redeployed. Robinson desired to remain in Serampore but seems to have been at least partially convinced by Carey to "choose a situation on the borders of Bengal where he might learn a new language & translate." Ward's counsel proposed Robinson to settle "on the skirts of Bootan, though in the Company's territory" and Robinson's fears, "seemed so much removed" that "he asked me to propose it to Brn. Carey & Marshman" (Smith, *Serampore Enterprise*, 104–5; Ward, Journal MSS, Monday, December 5, 1808, 679).

anything, I never published a page, without consulting him."[103] Of course, there is nothing of a uniquely Christian spiritual stamp in the fact that someone highly esteems friendship or even in someone's being a good friend—though we would certainly hope that, in varying degrees, these characteristics would indeed mark Christians. It was friendship of a Christian stamp that Ward prized in particular. For, it is only that friendship which exists between Christians on earth that will endure for all eternity. So, assuring a friend, presumably in England, that he would not forget him, he wrote concerning friendship:

> Oh! that we may be forming for that rational, sublime and eternal friendship, which befits the presence of God above. Why are friends severed? Why are friendships mixed with so many painful circumstances? If we are to die like the beasts, who can answer these questions? But if the light, which exhibits life and immortality, be the true light, and no delusive meteor, then we have an answer to these momentous enquiries—the house of friendship and of love is above.[104]

Conclusion

When Ward suddenly died of cholera on March 7, 1823, the loss to the Mission was incalculable. According to Christopher Smith, Ward's death was an event from which their mission never really recovered. Thereafter, it was too much to expect much creative thought to flow from the pens of his survivors. This was most unfortunate because it meant that the Trio were unable to reach anything like their missiological potential. Ward had become the only one of them who appeared able to make much of a contribution to mission theology or theory, but it was all nipped in the bud.[105]

In a funeral sermon preached at Union Chapel, Calcutta, his long-time colleague Joshua Marshman lamented, "Our beloved brother was so endeared to us in every capacity, that had our feelings been consulted, we should never have suffered him to enter into rest but with ourselves."[106]

Nevertheless, Smith's comment that future missiological contributions were "all nipped in the bud" at Ward's death, though truthful, seems overly dismissive. Though numerous colleagues, wives, and children perished along the way, Carey, Marshman, and Ward were permitted by God to labor together in Bengal for shortly over 23 years and accomplish as much as they did. Ward's contributions to the Mission over this time span, were indeed much greater than merely those he made in the printing office. As an evangelist, pastor, mentor, author, draftsman, husband, father, friend, and counselor, Ward was an encouragement and blessing to all who knew him.

---

103 Marshman, *Life and Times*, 2:280–81.

104 Stennett, *Memoirs of the Life of the Rev. William Ward*, 114–5.

105 Smith, *Serampore Enterprise*, 223n129.

106 Stennett, *Memoirs of the Life of the Rev. William Ward*, 230–1.

Providence and pragmatism:
Early societal engagement of the Serampore missionaries

Peter de Vries

Peter de Vries worked with his wife for many years as social entrepreneurs in Kolkata, providing freedom to women trapped in the sex-trade. Since 2014 based in Serampore, they work as tour guides for the region. He has a special interest in colonial and mission history, and volunteers at the Carey Library and Research Center to catalogue and digitize its holdings. Peter has a Master of Theology degree from Laidlaw College, Auckland, New Zealand.

Introduction

> Bearer, pull off my boots … Bring me some hot water … Sir, it is almost ready. What? … it is not ready yet [?] … Sir, your slaves have committed a fault; let there be orders to forgive. Hirkarrah, pull the Bearer's ears. Let him remember not to do so again.[1]

Twenty-first-century readers may be surprised to find that this piece of Bengali prose, a teaching aid for young East India Company recruits, was written by William Carey, the famous nineteenth-century Baptist missionary. Why did he use the term "slave" for a servant? After all, Carey was a fervent champion of the abolition cause, who prayed daily for slavery's destruction and abstained from West Indian sugar, "cleansing his hands of its blood."[2] Did the Serampore missionaries not work tirelessly to stamp out inhuman Indian

---

1 William Carey, *Dialogues Intended to Facilitate the Acquiring of the Bengali Language* (Serampore: Serampore Press, 1815), 7, as quoted from Timothy George, *Faithful Witness: The Life and Mission of William Carey* (Leicester: Inter-Varsity, 1992), 110. Carey used the Bengali terms *golam* and *chakor* for slave and servant here synonymously. A *Hirkarrah* is a messenger. *Contra* George, these dialogues were meant to teach Carey's pupils at Fort William College, and not school children. For them he wrote *Itihasmala*, fable-like stories.

2 "[F]or several years he never engaged in prayer, … without interceding for … the abolition of the slave-trade" (Eustace Carey, *Memoir of William Carey, D.D. Late Missionary to Bengal, Professor of Oriental Languages in the College of Fort William, Calcutta* [London: Jackson & Walford, 1836], 49). The reference to sugar comes from William Carey, *An Enquiry Into the Obligations of Christians, to Use Means for the Conversion of the Heathens* (Leicester, 1792), 86. Popularized by William Fox in his twelve page pamphlet, *An Address to the People of Great Britain, on the Propriety of Abstaining from West India Sugar and Rum* (1791–1792). Also see Timothy Whelan, "Martha Gurney and the Anti-Slave Trade Movement, 1788–94," in *Women, Dissent and Anti-Slavery in Britain and America, 1790–1865*, ed. Elizabeth J. Clapp and Julie R. Jeffrey (Oxford: Oxford University

customs such as infanticide, sati, *ghaut* murders, and hook-swinging they observed during religious festivals?[3] William Ward, in his survey of Hindu customs, wrote that, "Domestic slavery ... is very common in India, *however mild*, ... In some parts of India, children are as much an article of sale as goats or poultry," and that it demands severe reproof.[4] Yet, apart from occasional social comments, there seems little evidence that they actively opposed this customary practice.

This article argues that, although the Serampore Mission seemed ideally placed to dictate its own agenda of social engagement, in truth, the missionaries often acted in dependence on the East India Company (EIC), and pursued philanthropy only as far as their evangelical connections would allow. They focused on eradicating female infanticide and tirelessly lobbied for the abolition of widow burning, but domestic slavery and the Company's opium trade were left to another generation. The primary aim being the translation and preaching of the gospel, their reluctant acceptance of domestic slavery seems to be more of a pragmatic than principled approach. Our purpose then is to uncover the "real" Serampore Trio,[5] to peel away the layers of hagiography, and to use their transcripts to better understand the movement they initiated. Their relationship with the EIC was often tenuous, causing spiritual-secular entanglements that pulled them in opposing directions when threatened. From the outset, the missionaries would claim the Reformation principle, *Sola Scriptura*, as guide and called upon Providence to overcome these challenges. However, the reality was closer to a balancing act between idealism and pragmatism.

This article limits itself to two decades from the uncertain start of Protestant mission in Bengal (1792) to the passing of the Charter Renewal Bill (1813), the dawn of legitimate mission; the period in which the unlicensed missionaries were particularly under the scrutiny of cautious Company officials. Under the governance of Warren Hastings (1732–1818), Earl Cornwallis (1738–1805), John Shore (1751–1834), Richard Wellesley (1760–1842), George Barlow (1762–1847), and Lord Minto (1751–1814), the evangelical movement in Britain produced some remarkable advocates in the East, which began to transform a company of mercenary mercantilists into one of reluctant imperialists. While the historiographical debate surrounding the confluence of evangelicalism, abolitionism, and British expansionism is complex and ongoing, the focus here is to track the development of evangelical praxis in the East.[6]

Press, 2011), 57–58.

3 Sati, the practice of burning the widow on her husband's funeral pyre. *Ghaut* murders, the custom of leaving old or sick people to die at the steps (*ghats*) along the river. Self-chastising, the swinging on ropes of poles attached to the skin by hooks was promoted during the yearly *Charak (Churuck) Puja*.

4 William Ward, *A View of the History, Literature, and Mythology of the Hindoos* (London: Black, Kingsbury, Parbury and Allen, 1820), 3:281, 309. Emphasis mine.

5 Traditionally, the term "Serampore Trio" describes the close partnership between the co-directors of the Serampore Mission: William Carey, Joshua Marshman and William Ward, from 1800 to 1823. Here I have substituted "Trio" by "Associates" to include the efforts of the missionary wives. A. Christopher Smith, *The Serampore Mission Enterprise* (Bangalore: Centre for Contemporary Christianity, 2006), xx, 3n2.

6 The terms "evangelical" and "evangelicalism" describe the transatlantic revival movements as a whole, while the capitalized "Evangelical" refers to the Anglican branch of the movement. See Mark Hutchinson and John Wolffe, *A Short History of Global Evangelicalism* (Cambridge: Cambridge University Press, 2012), 6. In October 1757, Thomas Haweis, a young Cornishman, was

Evangelical ideals

> Boosy, this is a good country; that is, it would be a very good country, if the people were Christians. Then they would not be so idle as they now are and they would agree together, and clear the jungles, and build churches to worship God in. It will be pleasant to see the people … reading … God's book.[7]

Originally written in 1813 for children living in Indian military cantonment towns, Mary Sherwood's (1775–1851) best-selling tale of *Little Henry and His Bearer* (1814) exemplified the evangelical ideals of the late Hanoverian period.[8] Little Henry, the sickly hero of the story, reaches out with such wisdom, piety, and resolve that his faithful Hindu caregiver Boosy comes to accept the Christian faith after Henry's tragic but Christian death. The central character represents both the saintly scholar Henry Martyn (1781–1812) of Truro, Mary's much admired friend from her days stationed at Cawnpore, as well as her eldest son, Henry, who died in infancy.[9] The narrative revolves around evangelical themes such as original sin, salvation through Christ alone, prayer, Bible reading, witness, and Christian civilization––such as providing work, clearing forests, and building churches––as the solution to India's evils.

While Sherwood's stories are meant to inspire a young generation to missionary action, contrary to Dara Regaignon, *Little Henry* does not promote an Anglicized British society as the ideal. At the end of the story, Boosy is reading the *shasters* (holy books) with the help of Mr Smith in Hindustani, not English.[10] While it may display a typical evangelical

---

ordained to the curacy of St Mary Magdalen church in Oxford. Haweis's ministry rapidly stirred strong reactions. According to Charles Wesley, a co-founder of Methodism, he preached 'Christ crucified, with amazing success', and drew large crowds both from the University and the city. On the other hand, students jeered Haweis in the street, shouting 'There goes the saver of souls!': stones were thrown through the church windows while he was preaching, and 'This is the back way to Hell' was chalked on the church doors. More orderly, but ultimately more effective, critics eventually forced Haweis to leave Oxford in 1762. Not to be repressed, Haweis subsequently published a selection of the sermons he had delivered in Oxford under the overall title of Evangelical Principles and Practice. It was one of earliest attempts systematically to set out the theological outlook of the developing evangelical movement and its implications for Christian devotion and practice. Haweis's starting point was 'The Divinity of the SON and SPIRIT, co-eternal and co-equal with the FATHER'. He affirmed 'the inability of man in his fallen state to do any thing but evil' and the impossibility of human compliance with God's Law." Also see David Hempton, "Evangelicalism and Reform, c.1780–1832," in *Evangelical Faith and Public Zeal: Evangelicals and Society in Britain, 1780–1980*, ed. John Wolffe (London: SPCK, 1995), 17–37.

7 This story first appeared anonymously in 1814, but was later attributed to Mrs Sherwood, who lived in Bengal from 1804 to 1816. On the success of *Little Henry*, she became a popular children's book author. [Mary Martha] [Sherwood], *The History of Little Henry and His Bearer*, 8th ed. (London: F. Houlston and Son, 1816), 76–77.

8 The late Hanoverian period refers to the British period of political stability under George III (1738–1820) and IV (1762–1830), i.e. 1760–1830, prior to the Victorian era. *Contra* Smith, *The Serampore Mission Enterprise*, xx, fn 2.

9 Though technically a chaplain for the EIC, Henry Martyn was "a missionary in terms of his self-understanding and *modus operandi*." As translator of the New Testament into Hindustani (Urdu), Persian, and Arabic, his life was hugely inspirational. His close friend John Sargent (1780–1833) published Martyn's *Memoir* as early as 1819, which inspired many to missionary service. See Clinton Bennett, "The Legacy of Henry Martyn," *International Bulletin of Mission Research* 16.1 (1992): 10.

Barbara Eaton, *Letters to Lydia: "Beloved Persis"* (Penzance: Hypatia, 2007), 292, 303. Eaton points out that Mr Smith alludes to David Brown (1763–1812), one of the "pious chaplains" who resided for twenty-five years in India (Eaton, *Letters to Lydia*, 85), Henry Martyn's mentor who first introduced him into the study of Hindustani (Urdu). Mr Baron, "a very pious young man" (Eaton, *Letters to Lydia*, 59), refers to Joseph Parson (1780–1835), the Sherwood's evangelical chaplain at Berhampore.

10 Dara Rossman Regaignon, "Intimacy's Empire: Children, Servants, and Missionaries in Mary Martha Sherwood's 'Little

worldview, abounding in "overt religious and cultural propaganda, which places ... little Henry ... as morally superior to ... heathen bearer Boosy," Henry's pleasure-seeking English foster mother needs to be regenerated all the same.[11] Importantly, *Little Henry* exemplifies the belief in the necessity of inner conversion as a prerequisite to societal reformation, which, evangelicals believe, can only take place through effective diffusion of Christian knowledge.

Sherwood's missionary enthusiasm came at a time when established evangelicalism in Britain gained greater moral influence over EIC affairs. With their origins in a wave of religious Pietist "awakenings" from the 1730s spanning the English-speaking north Atlantic world, evangelicalism emerged to describe the beliefs and praxis of the revival movement.[12] Their publications, like the *Evangelical Magazine*, crossed denominational boundaries, seeking subscribers among those "persons of evangelical principles ... savingly converted to God, who trust in the merits of Christ alone for Salvation."[13] These forces of renewal drew upon and shaped the political and societal changes that accompanied the birth of the modern world, with its emphasis on (unlimited) reason, discovery, progress, and individualism.[14] Besides their emphasis on saving lost souls, evangelicals also showed a deep concern to promote a more humane society where Atlantic slavery would be uprooted.[15]

In their engagement with public issues, evangelicals objected to "a Christian society that is not Christian enough," protesting against societal irreligion, profaneness and disorder, the fruit of nominal Christianity.[16] They would, therefore, heartily support Governor Wellesley in Bengal, who, though not religiously minded himself, supported the Sunday observance, forbid gambling, set up a College on Christian principles and appointed two evangelical Chaplains. They would also agree with Wellesley's conviction

---

Henry and His Bearer,'" *Children's Literature Association Quarterly* 26.2 (2001): 89.

11 Eaton, *Letters to Lydia*, 297. Similarly, the description of the elaborate household in *The History of Little Lucy and her Dhaya* (1823) is better construed not as an imperial, but rather as a social comment on the extravagance of the British colonial establishment, employing *twelve* servants to wait upon Little Lucy.

12 Refer Bebbington's useful summary of four evangelical priorities: "*conversionism*, the belief that lives need to be changed; *activism*, the expression of the Gospel in effort; *biblicism*, a particular regard for the Bible; and ... *crucicentrism*, a stress on the sacrifice of Christ on the cross" (David W. Bebbington, *Evangelicalism in Modern Britain: A History from the 1730s to the 1980s* [Grand Rapids, MI: Baker, 1992], 1, 3).

13 "Preface," *Evangelical Magazine* 1 ([July], 1793): 2. Also see Bebbington, *Evangelicalism in Modern Britain*, 13. The Magazine was published monthly from 1793 to 1904, aimed at Calvinist Christians, and supported by evangelicals in the Church of England as well as nonconformists in the British Isles and New England. The phrase "savingly" pointed to the divine initiative in the process of conversion. Note that the Bible as its sole authority in the Magazine was assumed, and not yet specified.

14 David J. Bosch, *Transforming Mission: Paradigm Shifts in Theology of Mission* (Maryknoll, NY: Orbis, 1991), 262–7.

15 For instance, an anonymous author, writing under the pen name of Horatio, wrote: "The SLAVE TRADE, therefore, that infamous commerce in human blood, which has disgraced this nation for more than two hundred years; this trade, I say, must be relinquished, before the inhabitants of Africa will receive the Gospel" (Horatio, "Remarks on the Prophecies and Promises Relating to the Glory of the Latter Day," *Evangelical Magazine* 1 ([October 1793]: 164).

16 Andrew F. Walls, "The Evangelical Revival, The Missionary Movement, and Africa," in *Evangelicalism: Comparative Studies of Popular Protestantism in North America, the British Isles, and Beyond 1700–1900*, ed. Mark A. Noll, David W. Bebbington, and George A. Rawlyk (Oxford: Oxford University Press, 1994), 311; Chandler Robbins, "Extract of a Letter from the Rev. Dr. Robbins," *Evangelical Magazine* 1 (August 1793): 81.

that "Providence has admitted of the establishment of British power over … India, with any other view than of its being conducive to the happiness of the people, as well as to our national advantage."[17] Unlike most EIC officials, however, they were equally concerned for the spiritual and moral welfare of the Indian subjects.

Moreover, evangelicals put much emphasis on personal "vital religion," the active experience of God, which often was the sign of genuine conversion. They distinguished themselves between the ritualism and nominalism often found in the established church. The faith that sought ongoing transformation of their personal lives expressed itself in a corresponding public zeal seeking societal change.[18] Naturally, evangelical "zeal" was often frowned upon by the established church. The Evangelical movement would defend itself against the charge of religious "enthusiasm" and speak out against excesses of fanaticism. Yet, these suspicions were often difficult to overcome.[19]

Providence and Mission

The Serampore Associates made full use of the opportune time during the Wellesley's "grandiose rule" and were ideally placed to pioneer a new chapter in Christian mission.[20] However, they did not work in isolation, nor was their work unique. They learned from what other Europeans practiced, were shaped by it, and strove to apply it to the task of sharing the gospel. Whether translating, printing, teaching, engaging in Asian studies, botany or agriculture, they fostered a strong belief that God had provided Serampore as the ideal location for the myriad of activities they undertook.[21] Located in occupied Bengal, near Calcutta, the center of British influence in the East, the Associates used all their European connections to promote their cause. But their decision to identify with Company authorities would prove a two-edged sword.

Carey's reluctant decision upon the arrival of eight new missionaries, in October 1799, to move the Baptist mission from isolated Kidderpore in North Bengal, to the settlement of Serampore near Calcutta, appeared to be providential. Not that the circumstances were totally unexpected. Before they left, Secretary Fuller had sought the advice of Charles Grant (1746–1823), who recommended the new party seek asylum in the Danish enclave. Colonel Ole Bie's (1733–1805) hospitality and assistance were a sign of God's provision. Here was a Lutheran governor, who once enjoyed the ministry of the missionary Christian

---

17 Penny Carson, "The British Raj and the Awakening of the Evangelical Conscience," *Christian Missions and the Enlightenment*, ed. Brian Stanley (London: Routledge, 2014), 46.

18 John Wolffe, ed., *Evangelical Faith and Public Zeal: Evangelicals and Society in Britain 1780–1980* (London: SPCK, 1995), 2.

19 Stuart Piggin, *Making Evangelical Missionaries 1789–1858* (n.p.: Sutton Courtenay, 1984), 65–67.

20 While Carey stood at the beginning of a new movement, he is often wrongly given the epitaph "Father of modern mission" (Stephen Neill, *A History of Christian Missions*, 2nd ed. [London: Penguin, 1986], 222; Smith, *Serampore Mission Enterprise*, 1, 10).

21 In his Bengali translation, Carey followed Nathanial Brassey Halhed's (1751–1830) pioneering *Bengali Grammar*; in Sanskrit, the insights of Orientalist William Jones (1746–1794); in horticulture, he edited William Roxburgh's *Flora Indica*; in printing, Ward utilized the type making skills of Orientalist Charles Wilkins' (1749–1836) protégé Panchanan Karmakar (d. c.1804); in education, Marshman gleaned from Bell and Lancaster's Monitorial System. See Joshua Marshman, ed., *Friend of India* 1.3 (July 1818): 61–64; Smith, *Serampore Mission Enterprise*, 130–1.

Friedrich Schwartz (1726–1798) at Tranquebar, giving timely protection to the missionaries in the face of the British demand for extradition. All he desired in return was some official printing on their press, education for his children, their fellowship, and regular Christian ministry for his people.[22]

Serampore provided the fledging Mission not only much-needed legal status, but also unexpected respectability. It propelled Carey from a grass-roots evangelist into a celebrated College professor, Marshman from a village teacher into a writer-educationalist, and Ward into an accomplished printer and publisher. Serampore's progressive outlook even gave birth to Hannah Marshman's (1767–1847) revolutionary girl's education.[23] After the devastating yet strangely providential fire of the press (1812), which destroyed much of Carey's early work, their enterprise became so well-known that even William Wilberforce (1759–1833), the devoted Anglican MP, commended their efforts in his successful speech upon the Renewal of the Charter (1813).[24] At Serampore, dissent had become respectable, and the town prospered with it.

Throughout their lives, as was common among evangelicals and Calvinists, Carey and his companions looked upon divine providence governing their mission and commercial enterprise.[25] Their outlook stood in contrast to the prevailing deism of their day, which repudiated providence and divine revelation.[26] They would note each instance of provision with "What hath the Lord wrought!," as they sought to understand God's sovereign direction in all their decisions.[27] providence would open doors or forbid them moving forward.[28] In discerning the guiding factors, they attempted to understand the overarching divine purpose in each situation. If the circumstances would line up, such as their move to Serampore, this would be a sign of God's guidance. However, if trials, sickness and death would befall them, after much soul-searching and lament, they too would accept this as God's sovereign will. Such belief was not a mechanistic acquiescence to passive fate or secondary (accidental) causes, but a dynamic faith in God's active direction.[29] Carey's guiding principle in his decision-making was the extension of God's kingdom, by which all operations of providence would be "directed towards the end that the earth should be

---

22 Brunsdon to Sutcliff, December 5, 1799, in Carey, *Memoir of William Carey*, 367, 370.

23 The first girls' classes began at Serampore in 1816–1817, followed by the LMS Missionary Robert May's (1788–1818) girls' school at nearby Chinsurah (1818). Michael A. Laird, *Missionaries and Education in Bengal, 1793–1837* (Oxford: Clarendon, 1972), 133–4.

24 William Wilberforce, *Substance of the Speeches of William Wilberforce, Esq. on the Clause in the East-India Bill for Promoting the Religious Instruction and Moral Improvement of the Natives of the British Dominions in India* (London: John Hatchard, 1813); John Clark Marshman, *The Life and Times of Carey, Marshman, and Ward: Embracing the History of the Serampore Mission* (London: Longman, Brown, Green, Longmans, & Roberts, 1859), 2:23–29.

25 For instance, there are 36 references to providence in the *Evangelical Magazine* in the year of 1793.

26 Smith, *Serampore Mission Enterprise*, 257.

27 George Smith, *The Life of William Carey: Shoemaker and Missionary*, 2nd ed. (London: John Murray, 1887), 585.

28 See, for example, Terry G. Carter, ed., *The Journal and Selected Letters of William Carey* (Macon, GA: Smyth & Helwys, 2000), 17, 39, 48, 101, 139, 195, 197.

29 For a good overview on his view on trials and providence, see William Carey, Letter to Sisters, October 24, 1818, CLRC, mss copy.

full of the knowledge of the Lord."[30]

Carey would draw upon insights from John Flavel's (c.1627–1691) popular treatise *Divine Conduct, or The Mystery of Providence* (1677).[31] Written by an influential Puritan, this little book demonstrates the workings of providence personified like Lady Wisdom in the book of Proverbs, guiding the pilgrim along life's journey.[32] Flavel first notes that God manifests himself through the written word, and that the occurrences of special providence are his glorious works, the express fulfillment of scripture. He then exhorts Christians to find pleasure in observing "the mysterious workings of Providence … the execution of God's decree" in their lives, to see it accomplishing its purpose, which is holiness.[33] Dark and afflictive Providences may chasten the best Christian to "suffer but a while," but "no stroke or calamity upon the people of God can *separate* them from Christ."[34] In each hardship the Christian is encouraged to wait patiently and persevere cheerfully, in expectation that all things ultimately work together for good.[35] In a Puritan fashion, Flavel exhorts Christians to observe the mysterious working of providence as a prerequisite for constant spiritual renewal.

Carey learned these foundational lessons in "Leadings of Providence" during the bewildering circumstances around his and John Thomas' (1757–1801) departure in 1793. Evicted from the *Oxford*, he wrote: "All I can say in this affair is that however the mysterious the leadings of Providence are, I have no doubt but they are superintended by an infinitely wise God."[36] The whirlwind of providential events that led to the entire family sailing on the Danish *East Indiaman* and upon arrival after many uncertain wanderings to find shelter in Charles Short's (d. 1802) home only served to reinforce Carey's faith in the "all-sufficiency of God and the stability of his promises."[37] Faith in the ultimate sovereignty and wisdom of God became Carey's guiding principle, even as the path of Providence at times remained perplexingly inscrutable.[38]

In a similar vein, the Associates attributed to providence their timely arrival under

---

[30] Carey begins and ends his *Enquiry* with a reference to the coming of Christ's Kingdom. Travis L. Myers, "Tracing a Theology of the Kingdom of God in William Carey's Enquiry: A Case Study in Complex Mission Motivation as Component of 'Missionary Spirituality,'" *Missiology: An International Review* 40.1 (2012): 37–47. Smith, *Serampore Mission Enterprise*, 257.

[31] Originally published in 1677 under much longer title, reprinted in 1820 as, John Flavel, *Divine Conduct; or, The Mystery of Providence* (London: L.B. Seeley, 1824). Carey's *Journal* has three references to Flavel. His writings also show influence of the chapter "Mysteries of Providence" by fellow Baptist elder, Robert Hall, *Help to Zion's Travellers: Being an Attempt to Remove Various Stumbling Blocks out of the Way, Relating to Doctrinal, Experimental, and Practical Religion* (London: Whittingham & Rowland, 1815), 171–81.

[32] See Prov 1:20, which states that "The openings of providence, or rather the loud calls of providence." Carey to Ryland, November 17, 1813, in Carter, ed., *Journal and Letters of William Carey*, 287.

[33] Flavel, *Divine Conduct*, 6, 154.

[34] 1 Pet 5:10, Rom 8: 35, see Flavel, *Divine Conduct*, 222.

[35] Rom 8: 28, see Flavel, *Divine Conduct*, 9, 124.

[36] Carey, *Memoir of William Carey*, 89, 122.

[37] Carey's Journal, January 17, 1794, in Carter, ed., *Journal and Letters of William Carey*, 9.

[38] "I have been reading Flavel on Providence lately; but under every new shadow of a Trial, I find myself to be a learner" (Journal entry for February 4, 1795, in Carey, *Memoir of William Carey*, 217); "the ways of God are inscrutable" (Carey, *Memoir of William Carey*, 336).

Bie's protection, just before the British troops declared war on Denmark, taking possession of Serampore; "it was so clearly the leading of Divine Providence, that no one of us can entertain the shadow of doubt respecting it."[39] William Grant's removal, however, three weeks after their arrival, "was a very afflicting providence to us; but no doubt it was done in infinite wisdom."[40] Such tests of faith in God's providential pattern became increasingly common. Upon the heavy blow of the fire that destroyed part of the Mission Press in 1813, Carey refused to give in to despondency, trusting that "He will, no doubt, bring good of this evil, and make it the occasion of promoting his interest" even though, "to us, at present, the providence is exceedingly dark."[41] In their responses to tribulations, therefore, the Associates alternated between despondent submission to the all-wise and ever-loving God, and a hope-against-hope reasoning to provide some poise in the midst of confusion and pain.[42] Yet, a year later Carey rejoices that thanks to the overwhelming generosity of sympathisers, the rebuilt printing office is in a much better condition than before the fire, proving once again the inscrutability of divine providence.[43]

Since acting against providence was to forfeit the blessing of God, decisions were only taken after much soul searching.[44] Upon being offered the Bengali Professorship at College Fort William, Carey agonized, "Providence appears to put me in such situations as require the greatest abilities, the maturest judgement, and the most patient and persevering spirit."[45] It was only after careful consultation and concerted prayer with his companions that Carey accepted the call "with fear and trembling," assured by Brown and Buchanan that the mission would be "furthered" by it.[46] Carey's comment to Fuller shows that they realized this decision would greatly impact the future of the mission. As a dutiful civil servant of the EIC, Carey would need to assess each consequence threatening the survival of the mission in light of this momentous resolution. Constantly captivated by God's sovereignty, the Associates had an extraordinary ability to turn discouragements into opportunities of renewed faithfulness.[47] However, such constant resorting to providence would also put them in the eyes of younger associates above criticism. This led them eventually to break away and begin their own mission.[48]

---

39 Carey to Fuller, February 5, 1800, in Carey, *Memoir of William Carey*, 391.

40 Carey to his sisters, January 17, 1800, in Carey, *Memoir of William Carey*, 382.

41 "Through divine mercy no lives were lost" (Carey to Eustace, March 12, 1812, in Carey, *Memoir of William Carey*, 522).

42 Smith, *Serampore Mission Enterprise*, 261.

43 "His dealings have been such as to excite holy fear and awe on the one hand, and holy joy and triumph on the other" (Carey to Fuller, May 5, 1813, in "Extract of a Letter from Dr. Carey to the Rev. Mr. Fuller," *Evangelical Magazine* 22 [October 1814]: 407). "Divine Providence has done more than the most sanguine person could have expected" (Carey to Hall, August 31, 1813, in "Dr. Carey to Mr. R. Hall, Aug. 31, 1813," *Evangelical Magazine* 22 [October 1814]: 498).

44 William Yates recalls Carey's condemnation of his move to Calcutta. Yates to Fuller, September 1815, in Smith, *Life of William Carey*, 252.

45 Carey to Fuller, June 15, 1801, in Carey, *Memoir of William Carey*, 450.

46 Carey, *Memoir of William Carey*, 205.

47 Brian Stanley, *The History of the Baptist Missionary Society, 1792–1992* (Edinburgh: T&T Clark, 1992), 38.

48 See "Pretexts were never wanting when a brother was to be sent to begin a new station; 'a door in Providence' usually opened before him … it was his own fault if he did not succeed" (William Johns, *The Spirit of the Serampore System, as It Existed*

Mission under duress

Despite the advantages of Serampore, Carey was reluctant to move there, not only because of the substantial financial losses suffered upon Kidderpore's abandonment. He realized that with the institution of the Serampore Mission certain principles had to be sacrificed. One of them was independence.[49] To ensure its future survival, Carey, at the request of Brown and Buchanan, agreed to be appointed as teacher at College Fort William and come on the EIC's payroll, fully aware that the authorities would scrutinize their missionary activities. This decidedly pragmatic approach to mission had some important ramifications. Apart from a steady source of income, such tacit alliance, advocated to Fuller as timely provision, would not be seen as politically neutral by the Indian populace. It did not make the Associates immune from Company restrictions either. Those fears would be realized with George Barlow's arrival.

Alarmed by the mutiny of *sepoys* at Vellore (July 1806), of which it was rumored that missionary activities were to blame, Barlow suddenly ended the cordial relations between the Baptists and government.[50] While earlier recruits were able to stay, after the mutiny unlicensed missionaries were ordered to leave Bengal immediately. The eviction of Chater and Robinson was temporarily averted only because of the petition offered by the Danish Governor. Moreover, itinerant preaching and Bible distribution were now strictly forbidden because of real concerns that the rebellion was sparked by the Baptist's fund-raising for their Bible translations. This prohibition caused a real dilemma. If they acted in defiance, this would set precedent for a law against evangelization, which could finish the mission. On the other hand, if they yielded a little, and stayed quiet, the storm might blow over. Carey, upon the sound counsel of Brown and Udny, promised Barlow they would "conform to the wishes of Government as much as we conscientiously could," for their mission mandate could not be given up.[51] The Associates also urged Fuller to use his influence with Grant and Wilberforce "to preserve … the liberty to preach the Gospel

in 1812 and 1813 [London: Wightman and Cramp, 1828], 28).

49 Another principle they sacrificed was the Moravian ideal of a rural focus.

50 Penelope Carson, *The East India Company and Religion, 1698–1858* (Woodbridge, Suffolk: Boydell Press, 2012), 70–73; Stephen Neill, *A History of Christianity in India: 1707–1858* (Cambridge: Cambridge University Press, 1985), 2:149–50. This wide-ranging book charts how the East India Company grappled with religious issues in its multi-faith empire, putting them into the context of pressures exerted both in Britain and on the subcontinent, from the Company's early mercantile beginnings to the bloody end of its rule in 1858. Religion was at the heart of the East India Company's relationship with India, but the course of its religious policy has rarely been examined in any systematic way. The free exercise of religion, the policy the Company adopted in its early days in order to safeguard the security of its possessions, was challenged by Evangelicals in the late eighteenth century. They demanded that the Company should grant free access to Christians of all Protestant denominations and an end to 'barbaric' Indian religious practices. This gave rise to an unprecedented petitioning movement in 1813, comparable in strength to that for the abolition of the slave trade the following year. It was an important milestone in British domestic politics. The final years of the Company's rule were dominated by its attempts to withstand Evangelical demands in the face of growing hostility from Indians. In the end it pleased no one, and its rule came to a gory and ignominious end. In this compelling account, Penny Carson examines the twists and turns of the East India Company's policy on religious issues. The story of how the Company dealt with the fact that it was a Christian Company, trying to be equitable to the different faiths it found in India, has resonances for Britain today as it attempts to accommodate the religions of all its peoples within the Christian heritage and structure of the state. Note that Neill has the year of the Vellore Mutiny twice mistaken for 1807, not 1806 (Neill, *A History of Christianity in India*, 149, 150).

51 Carey to Fuller, August 26, 1806, in Carter, ed., *Journal and Letters of William Carey*, 89–90.

throughout India."⁵² Soon after, largely through the influence of Udny and Brown, these restrictions were eased somewhat. They could preach again in private houses but not in public, circulate Bibles but not tracts, in case they "would interfere with the prejudices of the natives," and itinerate into the country but not in an official capacity. Happily, they learned that no complaint against them had been received by the government.[53] The missionaries had been vindicated for now, but they continued to be under scrutiny.

The next occasion of alarm was the unintended circulation of a Persian Pamphlet critical of Mohammed that came to Minto's notice (1807). When Carey was confronted with it, he was shocked but denied any wrongdoing other than it being allowed to put to the press without revision. Such admission of negligence was serious, but since only 300 copies of the tract had been distributed, and solely in the Calcutta area, the damage could be contained. Considering the recent Vellore massacre, however, Minto realized the potential for this incident to destabilize EIC rule. Upon further inquiries, he prohibited any preaching in Calcutta and ordered the removal of the press from Serampore to his jurisdiction.[54] The Associates now submitted a memoir in protest to show "the improbability of disturbances being excited by attempts to convert the natives," and to prove that Christian instruction of the "Gentoos" was in accordance with the 1698 Charter Renewal Act.[55] Since the Press was on Danish soil, and Governor Jakob Krefting Bonnevie (1814–1881) came to their defense, Minto relented.[56] Printing and Bible distribution hereafter continued unhindered, but pamphlets became subject to British censorship, checked for malicious content prior to publication. Adapting again to new conditions, the missionaries reluctantly complied with this regulation.[57]

While the Vellore insurrection was quickly quelled, in Britain, the cause for Indian missions came under increasing duress of the growing anti-missionary lobby. The legitimacy of Indian mission was brought to the public in a series of provocative pamphlets, which blamed the mutiny on missionary activities, questioning the Company's tolerance of unlicensed missionaries (1806–1808). This charge was effectively neutralized by Fuller, Grant, and John Shore (now Lord Teignmouth). Under the influence of Grant and Wilberforce's lobby, the Court of Directors declared they were not adverse of the

---

52 Carey and others to BMS, September 2, 1806, in E. Daniel Potts, *British Baptist Missionaries in India, 1793–1837* (Cambridge: Cambridge University Press, 1967), 177–8.

53 Carey, *Memoir of William Carey*, 483; *Periodical Accounts Relative to the Baptist Missionary Society* 3.17 (1806): 278. The Associates used the term "natives" for ethnic Indians and ethnic Christians without demeaning connotations the term has today.

54 Potts, *British Baptist Missionaries*, 185.

55 Carey to Sutcliffe, September 16, 1807, in Carter, ed., *Journal and Letters of William Carey*, 92–93; John Clark Marshman, *The Life and Times of Carey, Marshman, and Ward: Embracing the History of the Serampore Mission* (London: Longman, Brown, Green, Longmans, & Roberts, 1859), 1:309–11; Penny Carson, "The British Raj and the Awakening of the Evangelical Conscience," 50.

56 "The Danish Governor told us he would not suffer the press to be taken out of the settlement, and if the English proceeded to use force, he would strike the flag and surrender himself as a prisoner of war" (Carter, ed., *Journal and Letters of William Carey*, 94).

57 Carey to Fuller, October 1807, in Carter, ed., *Journal and Letters of William Carey*, 94.

propagation of Christianity in India, and Minto's censorship was expressly removed.[58] The debate continued unabated until, under the pressure of huge evangelical-driven outcry, the Charter Act (1813) was passed to give the Christian missionaries restricted liberties to carry out their aims.[59] Common sense and evangelical passion had won the day.

Pragmatism and mission

From 1808 onwards, the Associates used their renewed freedom to expand their network of mission stations to new areas under company control, but rarely dared to venture beyond British territory until after 1813.[60] Constantly under-resourced, their main focus gradually shifted from indigenous evangelism to ministry among Europeans in Calcutta and upcountry military cantonments, where they could rely on the support of sympathizing officials.[61] The Associates now increasingly adopted a pragmatic and, at times, uncritically partisan attitude towards British expansion policies.[62] In Carey's famous Sanskrit speech held in 1804 at Calcutta, for instance, he applauded Wellesley for training youths at his newly founded College, who "will extend the domain of British civilization, security, and happiness, by enlarging the bounds of Oriental literature, diffusing the spirit of Christian principles throughout the nations of Asia."[63] During Carey's long career as a College professor, several of his students--such as David Scott, Commissioner of Assam, and John Lawrence, commissioner of Punjab--rose to highly influential positions, doing much good for the Indian people.[64] However, as the Bible moved along with the flag, receptive mission fields like Bhutan and the Rajmahal Hills, outside British control or permission, could not be serviced.[65] An opportunity to turn to independent Rajahs and explore the possibility of a truly indigenous mission was therefore missed.

In his *Enquiry*, Carey had warned against Christianity falling into disrepute, pointing out the benefits of presenting the Gospel message without the trappings of Western

---

58 Potts, *British Baptist Missionaries*, 189–92.

59 Neill, *History of Christianity in India*, 2:153–5.

60 John Chamberlain was invited to reside at Agra (1810) "under watchful eye of the magistrate," and district Judge Smith at Sylhet encouraged Krishna Pal to begin ministry among the Khasis in Pandua (1813). There was an exception, Chater and Mardon sailed to Rangoon in the Burman Empire (1807) and afterwards to Ceylon (1812). See Smith, *Serampore Mission Enterprise*, 174.

61 Founding dates of Serampore Mission stations: Serampore (1800), Calcutta (1803), Dinagepore (1804), Cutwa (1807), Rangoon, Jessore (1807), Goamalty (1808), Digah (1809), Balasore (1810), Agra (1811), Nagpore, Colombo, Patna, Surat, Chittagong (1812), Sirdhana,* Java, Pandua, Ava (1813), Allahabad (1814). Serampore, Calcutta, Cutwa, Digah, and Sirdhana were the only five Indian stations that had European missionaries in 1814. Adapted from *Serampore Missionaries, Brief View of the Baptist Missionary Society* (Serampore Press, 1814).

62 Smith, *Serampore Mission Enterprise*, 168.

63 William Carey, "Translation of a Speech in the Shanscrit Language," in *The College of Fort William in Bengal* (London: T. Cadell and W. Davies, 1805), 176. George Smith, *The Life of William Carey D.D.: Shoemaker and Missionary* (London: John Murray, 1885), 232–4.

64 Potts, *British Baptist Missionaries*, 177.

65 Carey had visited Bhutan and the Hills and wished he could send missionaries to evangelize the Santals and Paharis. Carey, *Memoir of William Carey*, 262; Smith, *Life of William Carey*, 120. On Robinson's failed attempt to pioneer the Bhutan mission (1808), see Smith, *The Serampore Mission Enterprise*, 104, n.66.

civilization. For him a Moravian approach of a self-supported rural base away from European influence was the ideal. Thomas and he would observe first-hand the injustices people suffered, and attempted to alleviate them. Although Udny's indigo business at Mudnabatty never turned profitable and had to be abandoned by mid-1799, Carey saw its potential redemptive nature for the *ryots* in the face of unscrupulous planters. The exploitation of the laborers he had witnessed stirred him deeply, and with new missionaries arriving, Carey and Fountain planned a new indigo business on their own at Kidderpore, Malda.[66] As noted, events beyond their control overtook this redemptive model of growing indigo in rural Bengal. While the Associates' extensive literary labors at Serampore (translation, publishing and education) would employ large numbers of Indians, who received daily Christian input, it sheltered them from the plight of the rural poor. Maybe it was this realization, together with his discomfort to the Mission's acquiescence to "capitalist quasi-colonial policy," that drove newly married John Fountain back to indigo planting in the Malda district in May 1800, sadly to die there a few months later.[67] The Associates' hope that their junior and Indian partners would make up this deficiency did not easily eventuate. Carey would complain later that the comforts of the metropolitan life proved to be a snare to new recruits, who rarely ventured out beyond the confines of the city.[68]

Perhaps it was their urban focus on soldiers, prisoners and sailors that became the greatest hindrance to the reception of the Gospel among Indians. Balancing both the "press and pulpit" associated their mission with the irreligious conduct of Europeans.[69] To remove this offense, and with the reluctant approval of cautious Minto, they decided to promote "real religion" among English speakers at Calcutta by founding Lall Bazar Chapel (1809) and the Benevolent Institution for Eurasian orphans (1810). Such focus was not without success. The chapel became, over time, a mission sending church, and the Institution a source of supply for capable mission personnel.[70] However, these European-aligned institutions, together with their expanding base at Serampore, increasingly absorbed all their energies and resources, leaving little time to develop an effective cross-

---

66 Samuel Pearce Carey, *William Carey, D.D.: Fellow of Linnaean Society* (London: Hodder & Stoughton, 1923), 161, 163; Smith, *Serampore Mission Enterprise*, 248–50. For an excellent treatment of CMS missionary James Long's (1814–1887) efforts to assist *ryots* in their struggles, see Geoffrey A. Oddie, *Missionaries, Rebellion and Proto-Nationalism: James Long of Bengal* (Oxford: Routledge, 2014).

67 British hegemony during this time was *quasi*, i.e. neither colonial nor imperial. The EIC, in what was still largely autonomous Bengal, was being "drawn into creating a territorial empire" in dire need to raise additional revenue through taxation, hence the term. See Smith, *Serampore Mission Enterprise*, 251, n.46. The usual reason given for this move is concerns for his health, but his correspondence reveals that Fountain was increasingly uncomfortable with the course his peers are taking (Smith, *Serampore Mission Enterprise*, 164, n.2).

68 "To tarry long at Calcutta is highly injurious to the spirit of a young man" (Carey to Fuller, October 25, 1809, in *Periodical Accounts Relative to the Baptist Missionary Society* 4.20 [1810]: 86). Unfairly so, as argued by his nephew, see Eustace Carey, *Supplement to the Vindication of the Calcutta Baptist Missionaries, Occasioned by Dr. Carey's "Thirty-Two Letters," Dr. Marshman's "Reply to the Rev. J. Dyer" and Mr. John Marshman's "Review"* (London: George Wightman, 1831), 60.

69 "I have some reason to think that the press and the pulpit have not work'd well." Minto in his letter to the evangelical Director Perry Carson, "The British Raj and the Awakening of the Evangelical Conscience," 64.

70 On these institutions, see Edward S. Wenger, *The Story of the Lall Bazar Baptist Church Calcutta: Being the History of Carey's Church from 24th April 1800 to the Present Day* (Calcutta: Edinburgh, 1908).

cultural mission strategy, nor engage in new philanthropic pursuits.[71]

Living in colonial seclusion under perceptions of collaboration with a foreign power, the Associates' effectiveness gradually weakened, which affected their yearly baptismal statistics, showing over time fewer ethnic than European converts.[72] Despite the advantage of Grant's discreet influence as director and chairman of the Board of Directors, which was vital for the survival of the mission before 1813, they never fully realized the mission's evangelistic and philanthropic potential. Compared to other Indian missions, the Serampore mission had the advantage of very effective Indian partners who established indigenous churches, but most of these gains would be lost when the Serampore Enterprise collapsed under financial burdens in the 1830s.[73]

Evidently, the Serampore Mission's dependency on the EIC to provide remunerations for literary and educational services led to ambiguity, conflict and disappointment. As the Associates juggled their involvement in different spheres, the European world encompassing the EIC, the indigenous, i.e. Bengali, populace, as well as the expanding mission community, while at the same time relating to distant Britain, some of the tensions they faced were inevitable. With increasing entanglements of secular and spiritual concerns, and under pressure to conform to the demands of many partners, the Associates often felt overwhelmed. Yet, it is to their credit that, despite these challenges, they continued often with limited understanding, solving each problem they encountered by considering all the practicalities, while at the same time relying on Divine Providence.

Responses to Infanticide and Sati

During their early years in Bengal, both Thomas and Carey had first-hand experience of infanticide, *sati,* and *Ghaut* murders--the exposure of the sick and dying. Acting on evangelical convictions and strong humanitarian feelings, they often wrote to the general public to expose these practices as "gruesome" Hindu rites, seeking support to outlaw them.[74] The first opportunity arose when Carey was employed as a professor at Fort William. His trusted friend George Udny (1803–1879), now on the Supreme Council, requested him to conduct research into the practice of sacrificing female infants at Saugor

---

71 Such reflection was overdue in light of the prevalent caste system. Smith, *Serampore Mission Enterprise*, 190–6. Ward and Marshman made sporadic visits to mission stations in Bengal, but evidently Carey did not visit any stations after 1800, apart from Cutwa (Katwa) where his son William settled. See Smith, *Serampore Mission Enterprise*, 180.

72 The statistics of the period of 1800–1821 show a total of 1,400 baptisms, including 700 "natives," 400 Europeans, and 300 "other" (Eurasians). Serampore Missionaries, "Reply of the Serampore Missionaries to the Attack Made in No III of the Oriental Magazine" (Serampore Press, 1824), 12. Further research is required to confirm this correlation. See Smith, *Serampore Mission Enterprise*, 283–5; Marshman, *Friend of India* 1 (1818): 2.

73 For an attempt to trace the ministry of ethnic Bengali preachers, see Eleanor Jackson, "From Krishna Pal to Lal Behari Dey: Indian Builders of the Church in Bengal, 1800–1894," in *Converting Colonialism: Visions and Realities in Mission History, 1706-1914,* ed. Dana L. Robert (Grand Rapids, MI: Eerdmans, 2008), 166–205.

74 John Thomas published first-hand suttee accounts in two Calcutta newspapers in 1789, urging for Government intervention. See Arthur C. Chute, *John Thomas: First Baptist Missionary to Bengal, 1757–1801* (Halifax, NS: Baptist Book and Tract Society, 1893), 25. For Carey's first observation of infanticide, published in the Baptist *Periodical Accounts,* refer Carey's Journal, July 9 to August 4, 1794, in Carter, ed., *Journal and Letters of William Carey,* 37; Carey, *Memoir of William Carey,* 187, 580. For his description of *sati,* see Carey to Ryland, Mudnabatty, April 1, 1799, in Carter, ed., *Journal and Letters of William Carey,* 79–80.

Island. With evidence of Carey's report, and perhaps with knowledge of the precedence set by Jonathan Duncan (1756–1811), the beneficent Governor of Bombay who had banned infanticide among the Rajpoots of Benares, Lord Wellesley moved swiftly to forbid the practice (1802).[75]

Encouraged that the prohibition was met without resistance, Carey utilized a network of trustworthy local informers to compile yearly statistical reports on Female Immolations.[76] In 1803, they found that within a radius of 30 miles around Calcutta, the number was in excess of four hundred, and in the six months following, over three hundred. These facts refuted the Orientalist Colebrooke's earlier conclusion that the practice was "rare."[77] With this information, Carey, together with his *pundits* at Fort William College, set out to prove from the Hindu holy books that *sati* was tolerated but in no way prescribed.[78] The Baptists would argue that *sati* was "in many cases more or less compulsory" and pushed to outlaw it. The authoritative Criminal Court, however, advised against abolition because it had religious sanction. Wellesley, now on the eve of his departure, confronted with the ambiguous nature of notoriously intertwined Hindu cultural and religious practices, remained undecided about abolishing *sati*.[79]

No progress was made while Barlow's attention was diverted to quell the Vellore Mutiny (1806). But, under Minto (1808), Carey reported that laws made to prevent infanticide and voluntary drowning had been successful.

> The report of the burning of Women, and some others, ... were made by me. I, at [Buchanan's] expense, made the inquiries and furnished the reports ... I have, since I have been here, through different mediums, presented three petitions ... to Government for the purpose of having the burning of Women and other modes of murder abolished; and have succeeded in the case of infanticide, and voluntary drowning in the river. Laws were made to prevent these, which have been successful. Lord Minto told Bro Marshman and me that a district in Goozerat had lately agreed to abolish infanticide.[80]

Despite these sporadic successes, the battle had only just begun. In light of the alarming rebellion of the Vellore *sepoys*, the question of *sati* was relegated to Parliament, which advised that it became "inexpedient" to interfere with religious customs. This diktat

---

75 Jonathan Duncan abolished infanticide as Resident of Benares as early as 1789, and as Governor of Bombay (1795–1816) in Kathiawar district of Gujarat (1808). John Wilson, *History of the Suppression of Infanticide in Western India* (Bombay: Smith & Taylor, 1855), 85. In light of Duncan's achievements, compare Marshman's surprising observation of Carey's effort: "This was the first instance of any interference by the British Government with the religious observances of the natives, and the first vindication of the principles of humanity in opposition to the superstitious feelings of the people" (Marshman, *Life and Times*, 1:158–59; Smith, *Life of William Carey*, 281–6; Potts, *British Baptist Missionaries*, 140–1).

76 For Carey's report on *sati* of 1804, see Claudius Buchanan, *Christian Researches in Asia: With Notices of the Translation of the Scriptures Into the Oriental Languages*, 2nd ed. (London, 1811), 35–37.

77 Potts, *British Baptist Missionaries*, 145.

78 Marshman, *Life and Times*, 1:222.

79 Carson, *East India Company and Religion*, 61; Marshman, *Life and Times*, 2:399.

80 Carey to Ryland on April 17, 1808, in Smith, *Life of William Carey*, 280–1; Carter, ed., *Journal and Letters of William Carey*, 82.

enforced the age-old EIC policy of strict neutrality in religious matters out of fear of commotion. In the case of the Vellore insurrection, not unjustifiably so.

Even so, the EIC's position of religious neutrality became increasingly untenable as the campaign to abolish *sati* moved into the public realm. The graphic nature of *sati* lent itself to stirring the consciousness of the nation and forcing the EIC to do more to Christianize and civilize the people under its care. Publications like Buchanan's *Researches*, together with first-hand eyewitness reports and Baptist statistics lent authority to Wilberforce's convincing speech on the renewal of the Company Charter (1813).[81] After restrictions on the Press were temporarily lifted, the first number of the Quarterly *Friend of India* contained an essay on the burning of widows, which would afterward be quoted as "a powerful and convincing statement of the real facts and circumstances of the case" and added to the growing body of literature that finally led the resolute governor Bentinck to prohibit *sati* in 1829.[82]

Responses to Slavery

In contrast to the unrelenting *sati* campaign, Indian slavery hardly received any notice. Although Carey's occasional comments indicated his strong condemnation, the issue of coerced labor had a much lower priority.[83] Initially blind to the extent of the problem, he somewhat naively wrote, "there are no slaves allowed in this country. The inhabitants are as free as in England, for what I see, and are paid their full earnings."[84] Perhaps his comment reveals that he had not witnessed forced labor first-hand in North Bengal. Had he made further enquiries, he may have learned of children being sold into slavery. Evidentially, Carey's awareness of Indian slavery improved over time. Yet, the sparse references in the publications of Grant, Buchanan, and Ward also show that Indian slavery did not get the attention that *sati* did.[85] There are many underlying causes for their reservation.

---

[81] Wilberforce compares slave trade in the West Indies with superstitious practices (like *sati*), as argument for Indian education (see Wilberforce, *Substance of Speeches*, 52, 98).

[82] Joshua Marshman, ed., *Friend of Indian* 1 (1820): 332–52. Smith, *Life of William Carey*, 285. For an overview, see Kenneth Ingham, *Reformers in India 1793–1833: An Account of the Work of Christian Missionaries on Behalf of Social Reform* (Cambridge: Cambridge University Press, 1956), 44–46; Potts, *British Baptist Missionaries*, 155–7.

[83] Upon news that Felix rescued a condemned convict in Ava, only to employ him as servant, Carey wrote, "I abhor slavery, and shall this week write to him to give the man his liberty" (Carey, *Memoir of William Carey*, 514). In 1803, Carey urged his Dinajpur friend Cunningham, to go home and make arrangements to free the slaves of his estates in Jamaica he had just inherited (Carey, *Memoir of William Carey*, 210).

[84] Carey to Fuller, June 17, 1796, in Carey, *Memoir of William Carey*, 265. Also see "no Slavery [is] permitted in this country, but the Black Natives are as much protected by the laws as the White people" (Carey to his father, November 25, 1793, mss copy, Carey Library, Serampore). Was Carey referring to Lord Chief Justice Mansfield's famous ruling in 1772 that on English soil (and Bengal, which was now under British jurisdiction) no slave can breathe? See A.H. Oussoren, *William Carey Especially His Missionary Principles* (Leiden: Sijthoff, 1945), 191.

[85] "Most of the slaves in Hindostan (where they are used only for domestic services) have lost their freedom by the act of their parents [offering them for sale]" (Charles Grant, *Observations on the State of Society among the Asiatic Subjects of Great Britain [Written Chiefly in 1792]* [[Parliamentary Papers], 1813], 50).

The 1811 edition of Buchanan's *Researches* does not mention slavery at all. However, the 1819 edition comments on female slaves in relation to infanticide practiced in West India. See Claudius Buchanan, *Christian Researches in Asia: With Notices of the Translation of the Scriptures Into the Oriental Languages*, 11th ed. (London: T. Cadell and W. Davies, 1819), 47, 56. He regarded *sati* and Juggernaut more urgent than slavery (Claudius Buchanan, *The Works of the Rev. Claudius Buchanan* [New York: Whiting & Watson, 1812], 369).

While *sati* was easily identifiable, accurate information on slavery in Bengal was difficult to gather. Without an organized information network, the reliability of the casual informant could not always be substantiated.[86] Unlike the situation in South India, there was no evidence of agricultural slavery in Bengal. When distress sales occurred after a natural calamity, forcing desperate parents to sell their starving children, the practice was regarded as a commendable "social safety net."[87] Likewise, deserted orphans would become the 'property' of the caregiver. The issue of slavery was therefore a problem of both definition and complexity. EIC Chaplain William Tennant, commented in 1798 that "slaves in India are of many different descriptions, according to the manner in which they have been acquired. No less than fifteen legitimate methods of acquiring slaves are specified in the Eastern code; some of which are peculiar to this quarter of the world."[88]

Enslavement in pre-colonial India involved forms of bondage that varied in degree and implication for the enslaved and included terms like vassal, concubine, debt peonage, and bonded laborer.[89] Not only were the terms "slave" and "servant" used synonymously (as in Carey's *Dialogues* above), therefore blurring the distinctions, but the institution of bond service was inextricably linked with the caste system. As an ancient Indian economic and social institution protected under Hindu jurisprudence, that "though celebrated for humanity, pays but small regard to the natural rights of man," domestic slavery could easily be justified under the present status quo.[90] This was reinforced by Hindu laws that gave slaves certain protections that free but destitute villagers lacked. Slaves could be freed after a debt with interest was paid, or when they produced a male heir for their master.[91] To address slavery then, would risk upsetting the entire social structure, something the EIC would never allow.[92]

Using the yardstick of the chattel trade of the West Indies, the Indian variety was relatively benign. India knew no practice of one race exploiting another. Tennant would go as far as to say that "In general, the domestic slavery of the Hindoos, is attended with less

---

The Serampore publication *Friend of India* discussed slavery in 1823 and 1825, see Andrea Major, *Slavery, Abolitionism and Empire in India, 1772–1843* (Liverpool: Liverpool University Press, 2012), 248n5, 262.

86 See The *pundit* of Capt. Wilson, caught "guilty of interpolating his books and of fabricating new sentences." Buchanan, *Works of the Rev. Claudius Buchanan*, 266–7; William Tennant, *Indian Recreations; Consisting Chiefly of Strictures on the Domestic and Rural Economy of the Mahommedans & Hindoos* (Edinburgh: Longman, Rees, and Anderson, 1803), 1:154–5.

87 Major, *Slavery, Abolitionism and Empire*, 28. Such distress sales occurred during the Great Bengal famine of 1770, as witnessed by John Shore, in his early years in Bengal. See W.W. Hunter, *The Annals of Rural Bengal* (London: Smith, Elder, and Co., 1868), 26–27.

88 Tennant, *Indian Recreations*, 1:131; Major, *Slavery, Abolitionism and Empire*, 248; William Ward, *A View of the History, Literature, and Mythology of the Hindoos*, 3rd ed. (London: Black, Kingsbury, Parbury and Allen, 1820), 4:307; Nathaniel Brassey Halhed, *A Code of Gentoo Laws, or, Ordinations of the Pundits* (London : [s.n.], 1776), 156–7.

89 Major, *Slavery, Abolitionism and Empire*, 24, 33. See Abhijit Dutta, *Nineteenth Century Bengal Society and the Christian Missionaries* (Calcutta: Minerva, 1992), 84–87.

90 Tennant, *Indian Recreations*, 1:128.

91 Tennant, *Indian Recreations*, 1:133–4.

92 Major, *Slavery, Abolitionism and Empire*, 25. Major's observation that missionary publications were careful not to equate caste with class in order to maintain the social hierarchy back home. To condemn domestic slavery outright could have caused repercussions for the position of the working class (servant-master relationships) in Britain (Major, *Slavery, Abolitionism and Empire*, 268).

harshness, cruelty, or exhausting labour, than what results from the system among other nations. A stranger is seldom able to distinguish between a slave and any other member of a family."[93] Moreover, Tennant proposed, did the tacit acknowledgment of slavery in the New Testament not infer its continuance? The Serampore Associates would strongly deny such conjecture.

While the forgoing arguments have some validity, they do not fully explain the missionaries' silent acquiescence to slavery. Pragmatic as they were, their focus was simply elsewhere. As Andrea Major has argued, missionary discourse of the period emphasized issues that would best support their cause, in order to awaken British empathy and generosity. Indian forms of slavery stirred no sense of national guilt back home. The existence of reprehensible practices such as *sati*, hook-swinging and *ghaut* murders, however, ideally lent themselves to propagandist purposes. Moreover, these issues did not compete with the cause of the West Indian slave trade that became the abolitionists' sole focus. They both represented two extreme ends of human depravity in desperate need of redemption; the Atlantic slave trade was European-made, its counterpart *sati* Asian and inherited. In view of these urgencies, the missionary dialogue around domestic slavery "subsumed within the wider discourse of Hindu religious oppression that saw individual enslavement as relatively insignificant compared to the collective bondage of 'heathenism.'"[94] Therefore, the emancipation of Indian slaves could not be addressed until well after the campaign for the Atlantic slave trade was won.

Critical discourse on humanitarian issues was taken up again by Marshman's pointed editorials in the *Friend of India* from 1818 onwards.[95] With support from enlightened Bengalis and evangelicals in Britain, a new generation of missionaries would take up many of the humanitarian causes that remained.[96] It is this pragmatic approach to Indian atrocities, motivated by deep convictions of the sanctity of all human life, that marked the Serampore mission enterprise after 1800.

Conclusion

The extraordinary variety of activities undertaken by the Serampore missionaries did not come about accidentally or in isolation. From the outset their primary aim was to make Christ known to the Indian people. When that goal was under threat, their evangelical friends directed them to move from a rural based self-sufficient mission model to an urban

---

93 Tennant, *Indian Recreations*, 1:134; Major, *Slavery, Abolitionism and Empire*, 249.

94 Major, *Slavery, Abolitionism and Empire*, 250.

95 Though claiming to be non-political, Grant's advice to Carey (1821) reveals it took some creative license, "I wish … to submit to you… whether it is not expedient that a missionary should generally abstain from the discussion of topics of a political nature relative to India and its inhabitants," as quoted in Henry Morris, *The Life of Charles Grant : Sometime Member of Parliament for Inverness-Shire and Director of the East India Company* (London: John Murray, 1904), 340.

96 From 1830 onwards, the General Baptist missionary James Peggs (1793–1850) became a leading abolitionist speaking out against pilgrim tax, slavery and the Juggernaut car-festival. James Peggs, *India's Cries to British Humanity, Relative to the Suttee, Infanticide, British Connexion with Idolatry, Ghaut Murders, and Slavery in India: To Which Is Added Humane Hints for the Melioration of the State of Society in British India*, 2nd ed. (London: Seeley and Son, 1830). On early missionary responses to the opium trade, refer Jon Miller and Gregory Stanczak, "Redeeming, Ruling, and Reaping: British Missionary Societies, the East India Company, and the India-to-China Opium Trade," *Journal for the Scientific Study of Religion* 48.2 (2009): 322–52.

focused "patron-dependent" model.⁹⁷ This shift to civil service under the EIC resulted in political, cultural and religious entanglements that grew more complex over time, causing them to take up all kinds of endeavors that often competed with their original goal. Under pressure to foster cordial government relations while maintaining a growing mission establishment, their ability to connect with grassroots Indian life came under pressure. Juggling being both *sahibs* and *sadhus* proved problematic too, which became apparent in disappointing conversion rates over time.⁹⁸

Undoubtedly the Associates attempted too much. They pursued a holistic gospel. But their herculean translation and educational efforts competed with the philanthropic engagement they were so passionate about. Impeded by institutionalizing forces, they risked missing God-given opportunities to explore receptive fields and to speak up on behalf of the enslaved. The Associates had to make difficult choices as they grappled with the implications of Britain's colonial aspirations. Such struggles between a principled apostolic approach and the pressures of realistic pragmatism may have proved symptomatic for the Serampore Mission. Who are we to judge? Their example reminds the Church today that holistic Mission is first and foremost God's (*Missio Dei*) and that societal engagement must flow from a biblical understanding of the value of human life. In this light, mission efforts to alleviate modern-day slavery are commendable and deserve our wholehearted support.⁹⁹

---

97 Fuller warned against the "ditch of patronage" into which the Serampore Brethren had fallen, see Hugh Anderson, *The Life and Letters of Christopher Anderson* (Edinburgh: William P. Kennedy, 1854), 305.

98 Smith, *Serampore Mission Enterprise*, 13.

99 The issue of modern global slavery was popularized by Kevin Bales in his *Disposable People: New Slavery in the Global Economy* (Berkeley, CA: University of California Press, 2004). For Christian responses, see ministries such as International Justice Mission and Bridges 4 Justice.

The Serampore Mission and the Moravian connection

Samuel E. Masters

Samuel E. Masters (PhD, Southern Seminary) is a missionary in Argentina, author of *Redeeming Love Has been My Theme: The Life of William Ward*, and co-editor with Peter de Vries of a forthcoming commentary on the Serampore Form of Agreement.

In 1777, Moravian missionaries Karl Friedrich Schmidt, a preacher, and Johannes Grassman, a physician, arrived in Serampore. They settled in this Danish colony, just north of Calcutta because it was the only place in Bengal free from the control of the East India Company (EIC), which prohibited missionary activity. They studied the Bengali language and began translating the Bible. However, the Moravian policy of self-supporting missionaries limited their capacity for evangelism, and the rigid caste system prevented close interaction with the locals. The town's population included few Protestants, and the Moravians faced staunch opposition from Roman Catholic and Armenian Orthodox residents. Because the Moravians maintained a policy of abandoning unfruitful fields, they left Serampore in 1792.[1]

That same year, leaders of the Northamptonshire Baptist Association formed the Baptist Missionary Society (BMS). Their first missionaries, John Thomas (1757–1801) and William Carey (1761–1834), sailed for India the following year. The leadership of the Baptist work in India would eventually devolve on Carey, who settled first in Calcutta, then moved to Sundarbans, and eventually put down roots at Mudnabatty near Malda. In late 1799, a team of four missionaries, including Carey's future partners, Joshua Marshman (1768–1837) and William Ward (1769–1823), arrived and settled at Serampore. They chose Serampore for the same reason that had drawn the Moravians: freedom from the interference of the EIC. Carey would join them from Mudnabatty almost immediately, and the Serampore Mission was born.

Moravian Beginnings

The town of Serampore was not the first point of contact between the Baptist missionar-

---

[1] David A. Schattschneider, "William Carey, Modern Missions, and the Moravian Influence," *International Bulletin of Missionary Research* 22.1 (1998): 8–12; Joseph Hutton, *History of Moravian Missions* (London: Moravian Publication Office, 1923), 165; S. Pearce Carey, *William Carey, D.D., Fellow of the Linnaean Society* (London: Hodder & Stoughton, 1923), 185; E. Daniel Potts, *British Baptist Missionaries in India, 1793–1837* (London: Cambridge University Press, 1967), 5.

ies and the Moravians. Carey had long admired their example, along with that of Puritan missionaries in New England. In his *Enquiry*, Carey declared, "none of the moderns have equaled the Moravian Brethren in this good work."[2]

The Moravian Church's history as a force for world missions begins with Count Nicolaus von Zinzendorf (1700–1760). While a student at Halle, Zinzendorf likely encountered the Danish Halle Mission, which sponsored missionaries in Tranquebar, India. In 1722, Zinzendorf gave asylum to Moravian refugees who took refuge on his estate, where they established the Herrnhut community.[3] Discord plagued their hopes of reestablishing the ancient *Unitas Fratrum*. Zinzendorf intervened and guided the Herrnhuters in adopting the "Brotherly Agreement" covenant.

Under Zinzendorf's leadership, the Moravians became known for their intense personal piety, novel communal arrangements, ecumenical spirit, and remarkable missionary zeal. Despite their relatively small size, they began the first modern, large-scale missionary effort, sending representatives to the slaves of the Caribbean, the Indians of North America, and the Eskimos of Labrador. Notwithstanding the impressive achievements of their early years, difficulties arose, including dissension and rumors of scandalous behavior.

While the situation looked grim for several years following Zinzendorf's death, the Moravians were blessed with the solid leadership of August Gottlieb Spangenberg (1704–1792) over the international organization and Benjamin La Trobe (1725–1786) over the church in England. One Moravian historian recalls, "The era of Spangenberg began with measures to revive confidence in the Church and to restore its good name."[4] In England, under the leadership of La Trobe, influential evangelical leaders were gradually won over. The most significant factor in restoring the good name of the Moravians was the undeniable fruitfulness of their missionary efforts. Robert Gallagher explains, "By the time Zinzendorf died in 1760, after twenty-eight years of cross-cultural mission, the Moravians had sent out 226 missionaries and entered ten different countries."[5] These efforts brought the Moravians to the attention of the future founders of the Baptist Missionary Society.

Moravian and Baptist contacts

The Baptist Missionary Society was born at a time of significant cross-denominational cooperation among evangelicals. J.C.S. Mason has shown that John Newton (1725–1807) was influential in recommending the Moravians to the larger evangelical world.[6] Newton also developed a warm relationship with many of the Northamptonshire Baptists who would found the BMS.[7] Before his tenure in London, he ministered in Olney, where he fellow-

---

2 William Carey, *An Enquiry into the Obligations of Christians, to Use Means for the Conversion of the Heathens: In Which the Religious State of the Different Nations of the World, the Success of Former Undertakings, and the Practicability of Further Undertakings Are Considered* (London: Kingsgate Press, 1961), 62.

3 *A Brief History of the Moravian Church* (Raleigh, NC: Edwards & Broughton, 1909), 46.

4 J.C.S. Mason, *The Moravian Church and the Missionary Awakening in England, 1760–1800* (Woodbridge, Suffolk: Boydell & Brewer, 2001), 11.

5 Robert L. Gallagher, "The Integration of Mission Theology and Practice: Zinzendorf and the Early Moravians," *Mission Studies* 25.2 (2008): 185–6.

6 Mason, *Moravian Church and the Missionary Awakening in England*, 68–70.

7 See Michael A.G. Haykin, *One Heart and One Soul: John Sutcliff of Olney, His Friends and His Times* (Durham: Evangeli-

shipped with John Sutcliff (1752–1814), the pastor of the Baptist church in that town. He also maintained a mentoring relationship with the younger John Ryland, Jr. (1753–1825), who pastored in Northamptonshire and helped found the BMS.[8]

Newton advocated for the cause of missions in general. Mason points to a sermon preached by Newton between 1784 and 1785 that lamented the lack of missionary efforts in evangelical circles.[9] He held up the Moravians as a positive example: "The extent and effects of the labours of the *Unitas Fratrum*, compared with their circumstances and resources, must not be omitted on this occasion. They doubtless excite admiration, and thankfulness to God, in every serious mind acquainted with the subject."[10] The high esteem in which the early leaders of the BMS held Newton influenced their views of the Moravians.

Mason also suggests the intriguing possibility that Carey may have had direct contact with the Moravians. He provides a map of the South Midlands showing the significant towns in Carey's early life and ministry. The map shows seven Moravian chapels or preaching points in the same area.[11] Mason admits that his evidence is circumstantial, but it would help explain at least in part the origin of Carey's missionary burden.

While the direct personal contact the Northamptonshire Baptists may have had with the Moravians is uncertain, they undoubtably read their writings. In 1767, the Moravians published an English translation of David Cranz's (1723–1777) *History of Greenland* that gave an account of the Moravian mission in that land. In 1790, the Moravians began publishing their *Periodical Accounts Relating to the Missions of the Church of the United Brethren Established among the Heathen*. The first issue, released in 1789, contained reports and statistics from around the world. For example, among the "Esquimaux on the Coast of Labrador," a work begun in 1771, they reported sixty-three baptisms at Nain, Okkak, and Hopedale.[12]

Andrew Fuller (1754–1815) had considerable knowledge of the Moravians' work. This is clear from his book *The Calvinistic and Socinian Systems Examined and Compared* (1793). He mentions their efforts in Greenland, Labrador, and the Caribbean. He cites Cranz's *History of Greenland* and points to their positive example: "The views of Moravians, it is true, are different from ours in several particulars, especially in matters relating to church government and discipline; but they appear to possess a great deal of godly simplicity; and as to the doctrines which they inculcate, they are, mostly, what we esteem evangelical."[13]

---

cal Press, 1994), 75–81.

8 See John Newton, *Wise Counsel: John Newton's Letters to John Ryland Jr.*, ed. Grant Gordon (Edinburgh: Banner of Truth, 2009).

9 Mason, *Moravian Church and the Missionary Awakening in England*, 61.

10 John Newton, *The Works of the Rev. John Newton* (New York: Daniel Fanshaw, 1821), 4:364.

11 Mason, *Moravian Church and the Missionary Awakening in England*, 85.

12 *Periodical Accounts Relating to the Mission of the Church of the United Brethren Established among the Heathen* (London: Brethren's Society for the Furtherance of the Gospel, 1790), 16.

13 Andrew Fuller, *The Calvinistic and Socinian Systems Examined and Compared* (Boston, MA: Lincoln & Edmands, 1815), 50.

Once on the field, Carey and his colleagues at Serampore, Joshua Marshman and William Ward, constantly referenced the Moravians. For example, during a conflict between the missionaries and the colonial authorities in 1807, Ward suggested a "memorial" be sent to Governor-General Lord Minto. Marshman recalls, "He urged that the Moravian missionaries never omitted to cultivate a good understanding with the Governors, wherever their Missions were planted, by making themselves personally known to them, and explaining their plans of operation. Thus, said he, prejudices are disarmed, and the designs of enemies baffled."[14]

While they sometimes went against Moravian precedent, their example seems to have never been far from their minds. For instance, in 1801, Carey wrote to Fuller, "It has been the custom of the Moravians to give new Names to those who were converted from the Heathens. We had some consultations about it. I opposed it because I thought there was no connection between baptism and giving names but principally because it does [not] appear to have been the primitive practice to change the names of those who believed."[15]

Moravian influence is evident in the two defining documents related to the Serampore mission: the *Enquiry*, and the *Form of Agreement* that shaped the Serampore Mission on the field. Perhaps no example illustrates that influence more than the account of the founding of the Baptist Missionary Society in 1792. At a meeting of the Northamptonshire Association, Carey referred to the latest issue of the Moravians' *Periodical Accounts*, which he had brought to the meeting. It reported evangelistic fruit among the American Indians, in the West Indies, Tranquebar, and Africa. Carey appealed: "See what Moravians are daring, and some of them British like ourselves, and many only artisans and poor! Cannot we Baptists at least *attempt* something in fealty to the same Lord?"[16] The Moravians' missionary spirituality would shape the Baptist Missionary Society and the Serampore Mission in three areas: their ardent zeal, communal lifestyle, and cross-centered preaching.

The Moravians' Missionary Zeal

When Carey appealed to the Northamptonshire Baptists, he probably had access to the 1790 Moravian *Periodical Accounts*, where he would have read, "To the grace of God alone they ascribe the zeal and perseverance with which the work was begun and carried on. This enabled Missionaries to despise all hardships and sufferings, and gladly to meet reproach and death itself; thinking themselves amply rewarded, if, by their labors, a few were brought to the knowledge of a Saviour and the hopes of everlasting life."[17]

British Moravian leader Benjamin Latrobe (1764–1820) emphasized the Moravians' willingness to face death in the missionary cause:

> I cannot ascertain the number of those who within these forty years have been taken off in those countries, yet I can say with certainty, that a number far exceeding one

---

14 John Clark Marshman, *The Life and Times of Carey, Marshman, and Ward. Embracing the History of the Serampore Mission* (London: Longman, Brown, Green, Longmans, & Roberts, 1859), 1:321.

15 Terry G. Carter, ed., *The Journal and Selected Letters of William Carey* (Macon, GA: Smyth & Helwys, 2000), 173. "Not" is missing in Carter's edition, due to an error in transcription. See BMS Archives, Letter from Carey to Fuller, August 4, 1801, Reel 36, 183 (The Southern Baptist Theological Seminary Library, Louisville, KY).

16 Carey, *William Carey*, 90. Emphasis in original.

17 *Periodical Accounts Relating to the Mission of the Church of the United Brethren Established Among the Heathen*, 6.

hundred have thus fallen in the attempt of gaining some Negroes and Indians as the reward of the travail of Christ's soul. Yet others have always been found who have not only readily accepted a call, but have voluntarily and earnestly offered themselves to supply the places of those who were taken off in this service.[18]

Latrobe also wrote of a former slave who visited Herrnhut and told the story of his mother, who was still a slave in Saint Thomas and "would be glad to hear of the Saviour."[19] One of the brethren, Leonhard Dober (1706–1766), was so stirred that he offered to sell himself into bondage to carry the gospel to these people.

Latrobe pointed to the self-sacrifice of Christ as the motivation that drove Moravian missionaries. He wrote, "We hope that as long as this principle ruleth in the hearts of the Brethren, 'Christ died that we should live unto Him in the world,' there will always be found such willing servants of the Lord, 'who love not their lives unto the death,' but devote themselves entirely unto the service of their fellow creatures for Christ's sake."[20] He also called on other Christians to at least take up the burden of missionary intercession: "I am persuaded that all those who love the Lord Jesus Christ, and wish for the happiness of their fellow-creatures, will join in prayer, that the Lord of the harvest may continue to bless and prosper this important work, until 'the Knowledge of the Lord covereth the earth, even as the waters cover the sea.'"[21]

This exemplary zeal left an impression on Carey. In December 1797, he would write to the BMS from India: "With the Moravians none are yet to be compared either for Zeal—Labour—Perseverance—or success; but after them You were *the first* to engage in the God-like work of Missions. Your Zeal, worthy Brethren, hath provoked many others, to whose noble efforts we devoutly wish success."[22]

Carey understood this zeal had to be shared among the missionaries. He wrote to the BMS, "Your missionaries must be good men, who will not be intimidated at a trifle, or even at a very formidable appearance; men of prudence and tolerably good natural parts."[23] This reflects Carey's effort to follow the Moravians' example. On November 26, 1796, he wrote:

> More missionaries I think absolutely necessary to the support of the Interest, and should the Plan which I have proposed, and which must resemble that of the Moravians be judged eligible, it will then be absolutely necessary to pay the strictest attention to Missionaries and Missionaries Wives, being quite hearty in coming into the necessary regulations for the ordering of such a Family.[24]

In the same letter, he proposed that the missionaries have separate houses but share in one common stock under the administration of one steward. He envisioned a community

---

18 Benjamin Latrobe, *A Succinct View of the Missions Established among the Heathen by the Church of the Brethren, or Unitas Fratrum in a Letter to a Friend* (London: M. Lewis, 1771), 7.

19 Latrobe, *Succinct View of the Missions Established among the Heathen by the Church of the Brethren*, 15.

20 Latrobe, *Succinct View of the Missions Established among the Heathen by the Church of the Brethren*, 7–8.

21 Latrobe, *Succinct View of the Missions Established among the Heathen by the Church of the Brethren*, 32.

22 Carey to Society, December 9, 1797, in Carter, ed., *Journal and Selected Letters of William Carey*, 74.

23 *Periodical Accounts Relative to the Baptist Mission Society*, 1.5 (1800): 373.

24 Carey to Ryland, Mudnabatty, November 26, 1796, in Carter, ed., *Journal and Selected Letters of William Carey*, 137.

where all shared in the labor, minimizing the need for servants.

A Moravian-Style Community

On Saturday, January 18, 1800, Ward recorded in his journal the adoption of a set of rules for the Serampore family based on absolute equality. This represents the formal inauguration of the Moravian-style community. Each member shared equally in prayer and preaching. The administration rotated monthly, although Carey oversaw the medicine chest and the treasury. Fountain was appointed librarian. Saturday evening was dedicated to "the adjusting of differences, and pledging ourselves to love each other."[25] This agreement foreshadowed the more detailed covenant known as the *Serampore Form of Agreement* (SFA) that would be signed by the missionaries in 1805.

The *SFA* formalized the Serampore Mission's organization along Moravian lines. According to Samuel Pearce Carey (1862–1953), it deviated from the Moravian pattern in only one critical aspect. The Moravians held that each mission "should appoint a head for house-father, to whom the rest should in love be subject."[26] Carey explains that "Carey deliberately planned otherwise. Forgoing his own claim to headship or house-fathership, he founded Serampore on equality for each, pre-eminence for none."[27] In Carey's judgment, "the bold stroke paid off." However, the coming years would witness a tragic controversy that would cast a shadow on the Moravian pattern and its implementation by the Serampore missionaries.

The *SFA*'s eleventh statement shaped the Serampore community's communal lifestyle. Carey summarized it in this way, "To give ourselves without reserve to the Cause, "not counting even the clothes we wear our own."[28] This section included the following rousing defense of the Moravian approach:

> If we give up the resolution which was formed on the subject of private trade, when we first united at Serampore, the mission is from that hour a lost cause. A worldly spirit, quarrels, and every evil work will succeed the moment it is admitted that each brother may do something on his own account. Woe to that man who shall ever make the smallest movement towards such a measure. Let us continually watch against a worldly spirit, and cultivate a Christian indifference to every indulgence. Rather let us bear hardness as good soldiers of Jesus Christ, and endeavour to learn in every state to be content.[29]

This statement regarding missionary character seems indisputable. However, its application via a radical communal system eventually caused difficulties. The *SFA* states that

---

25 William Ward, *William Ward's Missionary Journal. 1799–1811*, ed. E. Daniel Potts (Typed transcription, n.d.), 1:66.

26 Carey, *William Carey*, 186.

27 Carey, *William Carey*, 186.

28 Carey, *William Carey*, 249. This is a useful summary. However, the first point only does partial justice to the theology expressed in the *Form of Agreement*. S.P. Carey was a sympathetic biographer but failed to grasp the importance of William Carey's theology. The *SFA* was originally printed at the Brethren's Press at Serampore in 1805. An edited version reprinted in the *Periodical Accounts relative to the Baptist Missionary Society*, 3 (1806): 198–211. The following quotes the London version with the Serampore version in brackets.

29 "The Serampore Form of Agreement," 211.

the communal arrangement was specifically instituted to glorify God and that God had shown his blessings on them as a result. The financial nature of this arrangement was to have "all things in common, and that no one should pursue business for his own exclusive advantage."[30]

The issue of character always seems to have been uppermost in the missionaries' minds. Early on, Ward recognized the arrangement called for unique people and he expressed his concern:

> So much depends on a man's disinterestedness forbearance, meekness and self-denial. One man of the wrong temper could make our house a hell. So much wisdom will be necessary. It is but here and there that one makes conscience of strangling thoughts, and of esteeming others better than himself. Only few are fit to live in such a settlement as ours is to be, where selfish passions must be crushed and the love of Christ swallow up all else.[31]

The Mission's daily affairs were left mostly in the hands of Joshua Marshman, William Ward, and their wives, Hannah Marshman (1767–1847) and Mary Ward (1773–1832). Over the years, as newer missionaries arrived, Marshman and his wife Hannah would become a focus of resentment. Carey spent large portions of his time in Calcutta teaching, working on Bible translations, and ministering at the Lal Bazar Church. He excelled at translating, and his time was well spent. However, some of the problems that developed might have been avoided, or at least minimized, had he given more definition to the leadership structure of the mission.

The Influence of Moravian Evangelism

The Moravians' spirituality centered on the crucifixion. At its best, the Moravians' focus created a great spiritual intimacy with Christ, communion with the brethren, and a driving desire to share the gospel with the world. However, during the period of declension that came to be known as the "Sifting Time," their spirituality was taken to almost medieval extremes by Zinzendorf and others. Graphically expressed in Moravian hymns and litanies, it became known as the "Blood and Wounds" theology. It included the "Litany of the Wounds," a hymn the Moravians deemed effective on the mission field. Moravian missionaries David Zeisberger (1721–1808) and Friedrich Cammerhof (1721–1751) "found blood and wounds language to be particularly effective" in communicating with the Mohican Indians.[32]

Putting its supposed effectiveness aside, extreme examples of this "Blood and Wounds" language shocked other European Christians. Craig D. Atwood catalogs some of the stronger statements,

> In the Litany of the Wounds, the wounds of Jesus are called "juicy" and "succulent" because they provide nourishment for the soul. The worshiper is strengthened by sucking at the side of Christ; he "licks it, tastes it." The wounds provide a warm and soft bed in which to lie. They protect children from the cold, so that the worshiper says, "I like

---

30 "The Serampore Form of Agreement," 211.

31 Carey, *William Carey*, 185.

32 Craig D. Atwood, "Understanding Zinzendorf's Blood and Wounds Theology," *Journal of Moravian History* 1 (2006): 32.

lying calm, gentle, and quiet and warm. What shall I do? I crawl to you." The believer longs to return to the womb, to crawl inside the "deep wounds of Jesus" and lie there safe and protected. The wounds were bloody and tasty, and spread the power of salvation over the believer. "Powerful wounds of Jesus, so moist, so gory, bleed on my heart so that I may remain brave and like the wounds."[33]

J.E. Hutton, a Moravian historian, criticized Zinzendorf's focus on the mere physical details of the crucifixion to the exclusion of its moral and spiritual value.[34] After Zinzendorf's death, Spangenberg and Latrobe backed away from the more extreme expressions of Zinzendorf's spirituality. For example, in the preface to the English translation of Spangenberg's *Exposition*, Latrobe wrote:

> True it is, that at a certain times particularly between 1747 and 1753 many of the Brethren, in their public discourses, and in the hymns which were published about that period, used expressions which were indefensible. The Count himself laboured to correct both the theory and language; and he was successful, and they are no more in use among the Brethren. The Brethren's congregations do not take the writings of the Count, or of any man, as their standard of doctrine; the Bible alone is their standard of truth, and they agree with the Augustan, or Augsburg confession, as being conformable to it.[35]

This more temperate tone and the undeniable fruitfulness of their mission work helped their influence grow. Fuller would write of their missionary preaching in favorable terms,

> The doctrine of atonement by the death of Christ, in particular, forms the great subject of their ministry. The first person in Greenland who appeared willing to receive the gospel was an old man who came to the missionaries for instruction. "We told him," say they, "as well as we could, of the creation of man, and the intent thereof—of the fall and corruption of nature—of the redemption effected by Christ—of the resurrection of all men, and eternal happiness or damnation." They inform us, afterwards, that the doctrine of the cross, or "the Creator's taking upon him human nature, and dying for our sins," was the most powerful means of impressing the minds of the heathen, and of turning their hearts to God. "On this account," they add, "we determined (like Paul) to know nothing but Jesus Christ, and him crucified."[36]

In 1793, Christian Ignatius Latrobe (1758–1836), Benjamin's son, would respond similarly to a Particular Baptist Missionary Society letter asking for advice. About missionary preaching, Latrobe wrote,

> When the Brethren went first among the heathen, they thought that they must first enter upon an explanation of the greatness, justice, omnipresence &c of God of the heinousness of Sin &c. but they soon found that "to know nothing among them save

---

33 Atwood, "Understanding Zinzendorf's Blood and Wounds Theology," 39.

34 Hutton, *History of the Moravian Church*, 276.

35 August Gottlieb Spangenberg, *An Exposition of Christian Doctrine: As Taught in the Protestant Church of the United Brethren* (London: W. and A. Strahan, 1784), vi.

36 Fuller, *Calvinistic and Socinian Systems Examined and Compared*, 50.

Jesus & him crucified" was the right way; the Word of the Cross, proved the power of God unto Salvation, and every other good thing followed.[37]

This advice from the Moravians was reflected in the *SFA*,

> In preaching to the heathen, we must keep to the example of St. Paul, and make the greatest subject of our preaching, Christ Crucified. It would be very easy for a missionary to preach nothing but truths, and that for many years together, without any well-grounded hope of becoming useful to one soul. The doctrine of Christ's expiatory death and all-sufficient merits had been, and must ever remain, the great means of conversion.[38]

That the Serampore missionaries had the Moravians' advice in view is confirmed by additional statements. As Ward writes in the *SFA*, "It is a well-known fact that the most successful missionaries in the world at the present day make the atonement of Christ their continued theme. We mean the Moravians. They attribute all their success to the preaching of the death of our Saviour."[39] The Serampore Trio largely took the Moravians' advice to heart. The wisdom of the approach was confirmed in their own ministry: "So far as our experience goes in this work, we must freely acknowledge, that every Hindoo among us who has been gained to Christ, has been won by the astonishing and all-constraining love exhibited in our redeemer's propitiatory death. Oh! then may we resolve to know nothing among Hindoos and Mussulmans but Christ and Him crucified."[40]

The preaching of the cross was always Carey's central concern. In 1794, before he had mastered the languages of India, he wrote in his journal,

> Through mistake spent this Day as the Sabbath. I have however abundant reason to be thankful for the mistake, it has been a time of refreshing indeed to me; O what is there in all this World worth living for but the presence and service of God-I feel a burning desire that all the World may know this God and serve him - O how long will it be till I shall know so much of the Language of the Country as to preach Christ Crucified to them; but bless God I make some progress.[41]

Two years later, Carey wrote a letter to his sisters that captured his passion and the specific content of his preaching,

> I preach every day to the Natives, and twice on the Lord's Day constantly, besides other itinerant labours, and I try to speak of Jesus Christ and him crucified, and of him alone, but my soul is often much dejected to see no fruit. This morning I preached to a number from "to know the Love of God which passeth knowledge". I was much affected myself, filled with grief and anguish of Heart, because I knew they were going to Idolatrous and Mohammedan feasts immediately after, this being the first day of the Hindu

---

37 C.I. Latrobe to John Rippon, London, 26 June 1793, in Timothy D. Whelan, ed., *Baptist Autographs in the John Rylands University Library of Manchester (1741–1845)* (Macon, GA: Mercer University Press, 2009), 65.

38 "Serampore Form of Agreement," 201–202.

39 "Serampore Form of Agreement," 202.

40 "Serampore Form of Agreement," 202.

41 Carey's Journal, March 29, 1794, in Carter, ed., *Journal and Selected Letters of William Carey*, 21.

Year; and the new Moon Ramadan of the Mohammedans. They are going I suppose to their Abominations at this moment, but I hope to preach to them again in the evening. I spoke of the Love of God in bearing with his Enemies, in supporting and providing for them, in sending his Son to die for them, in sending the Gospel to them, and in saving many of them from eternal Wrath.[42]

Years later, when Carey's son Jabez (1793–1862) began his mission to Amboyna in the Moluccan Islands, Carey's advice echoed the concerns he expressed in Mudnabatty. Carey wrote to him, "I rejoice that you have begun to preach in Malay. Consider this as your greatest work and labour to build up the people in Faith and Holiness, but above all labour to lay Christ Crucified as the foundation on which you build for all that is not built on that foundation will fail."[43]

The *SFA*'s fifth statement dealt with the cross's centrality in evangelism. As seen above, the Serampore missionaries distinguished between general "truths" and the specific message of the cross. They cited the Moravians as an example, but they also connected this approach to the Protestant Reformation,

> This doctrine, and others immediately connected with it, have constantly nourished and sanctified the church. Oh! that these glorious truths may ever be the joy and strength of our own souls, and then they will not fail to become the matter of our conversation to others. It was the proclaiming of these doctrines that made the Reformation from Popery in the time of Luther spread with such rapidity. It was these truths that filled the sermons to the modern Apostles, Whitefield, Wesley, etc. when the light of the gospel which had been held up with such glorious effects by the Puritans was almost extinguished in England.[44]

While acknowledging the influence of the Moravians, in their view, the message of the cross linked the first generation of Reformers with the Puritans, the later leaders of the evangelical Revival, and their own work at Serampore.

The Influence of Spangenberg

In January 1784, August Spangenberg wrote an introductory letter for a work published in English under the title *Instructions for the Members of the Unitas Fratrum, who Minister in the Gospel Among the Heathen*. He commented that fifty years had passed "since some of our Brethren first set out, with the view of carrying the gospel to the poor heathen; some in very cold, and some in very hot climates."[45] He confessed that "We had, at that time, no experience of the labour in the gospel." As a result, they were incapable of providing instruction. The best they could do was "commend them to the Lord, and the word of his grace." Spangenberg wrote the *Instructions* to remedy this problem.

---

42 Carey to Sisters, Mudnabatty, April 10, 1796, in Carter, ed., *Journal and Selected Letters of William Carey*, 85.

43 Carey to Jabez, undated, in Carter, ed., *Journal and Selected Letters of William Carey*, 255.

44 "Serampore Form of Agreement," 202. The quote follows the original Serampore version. The London version rephrased the reference to George Whitefield (1714–1770), John Wesley (1703–1791), and the Puritans as "most useful men in the eighteenth century," *PA* 3 (1806): 202.

45 August Gottlieb Spangenberg, *Instructions for the Members of the Unitas Fratrum, Who Minister in the Gospel Among the Heathen* (London: Brethren's Society for the Furtherance of the Gospel, n.d.), iii.

Numerous similarities exist between the *Serampore Form of Agreement* and Spangenberg's *Instructions*. While there is no direct evidence the Serampore brethren consulted the *Instructions*, certain similarities with the *SFA* are evident. Spangenberg's work is organized into numbered points like the *SFA*. In the *SFA*, the points grow progressively longer, and it is not always easy to see a logical progression between them. Frankly, the *SFA* seems to be a collection of brilliant ideas that need editing. The *Instructions* strikes the reader as equally brilliant, yet more orderly.

Similarities
Like the *SFA*, the first points of *Instructions* deal with theological foundations. As one might expect, there is nothing like the *SFA*'s evangelical Calvinism. Instead, the first point deals with the "great importance" of "preaching the gospel to the heathen." Spangenberg emphasizes that "whoever is employed" in the work of missions "is charged with an office of great trust; for he has to do with souls redeemed, 'not with corruptible things, such as silver and gold, but with the precious blood of our Lord Jesus Christ.'"[46] Spangenberg's second point simply restates the Great Commission and links it to the baptism of the Holy Spirit by which "they were prepared and endued with power, in an extraordinary manner, for this great work."[47] The third point cites 1 Timothy 2:3–4: "God our Saviour will have all men to be saved, and to come unto the knowledge of the truth." This is deployed as an argument that "the gospel be preached to the heathen."[48] The Serampore Trio would have agreed with the overall spirit of Spangenberg's defense of taking the gospel to the heathen, even if they differed in their commitment to evangelical Calvinist soteriology.

If anything, Spangenberg places even more emphasis on the role of women in the work of missions. The letter introducing the *Instructions* begins, "Dearly beloved *Brethren* and *Sisters*."[49] The opening paragraph states, "It appeared, in the process of time, that they could not be of effective service, without the assistance of some Sisters among the heathen women." The *Instructions* explains,

> For when people are truly awakened, they are very desirous to open all their circumstances, in confidence to some person, and to seek good advice. But if those of the female sex have no one to whom they can freely open their minds, except to one or another Brother, who resides among them; some unsuitable, if not hurtful consequences will follow. Therefore, to prevent this, it was determined the Sisters should accompany their Husbands, as helpers among the female heathen.[50]

Spangenberg underlines that the mission would be much less effective without women missionaries.

Like the *SFA*, the *Instructions* contains advice on missionary character and temperament. The book emphasizes that missionaries must be cheerful and poor in spirit. Section

---

46 Spangenberg, *Instructions for the Members of the Unitas Fratrum*, 1.

47 Spangenberg, *Instructions for the Members of the Unitas Fratrum*, 2.

48 Spangenberg, *Instructions for the Members of the Unitas Fratrum*, 2.

49 Spangenberg, *Instructions for the Members of the Unitas Fratrum*, iii.

50 Spangenberg, *Instructions for the Members of the Unitas Fratrum*, iii.

Nine of the *Instructions* is dedicated to this attribute: "'Well, then, I will not love my own life, but will boldly go in thy name, and upon thy word.' In this case we can freely say, such a one has chearfulness [sic] and freedom to engage in the service of our Saviour among the heathen … With the aforesaid chearfulness, poverty of spirit is closely combined in a faithful heart. It is the opposite to that rash spirit found in people, who know themselves as little, as the important work for which they are to prepare themselves."[51]

Several sections of the *Instructions* are dedicated to the personal qualities of the missionaries, and the individual holiness required. Point fourteen declares,

> Whoever desires to be a messenger of peace to the heathen, and magnify the grace of God in Christ unto them; his very countenance must bespeak the happiness of his heart: for if he does not himself enjoy peace with God, through our Lord Jesus Christ, if he cannot rejoice in God our Saviour, he will prove a very wretched messenger of peace. It is therefore necessary for us to 'experience daily anew, that we have in Christ Jesus, redemption through his blood, even the forgiveness of sins; and that we proceed in the ways of God from day to day, in full assurance, that the Father of our Lord Jesus Christ is also our dear Father.[52]

Again, like the *SFA*, the *Instructions* speak of the importance of preserving unity among the missionaries and being careful of the testimony the missionaries present by their behavior among the nationals. The *Instructions* advises that the "brethren take all possible pains to learn the language of those heathen, with whom they have to do. At times one or another is found among them, who is, in some measure, acquainted with the language of the Europeans, who trade with them."[53] Interpreters can be used initially but should not be seen as a replacement for learning the local language.

Many more points of contact exist between the *Instructions* and the *SFA*. Reading them side by side provides context for William Ward's exclamation, "Thank you, Moravians! Ye have done me good. If I am ever a missionary worth a straw, I shall owe it to you, under our Saviour."[54]

Differences
While the Moravians' influence on the *SFA* is evident, it is far from absolute. One notable difference involved the decision mentioned earlier involving renaming new converts. The Moravians followed the practice of giving converts Christian names. The *SFA* does not draw a specific contrast with the Moravians, but, as already seen, in 1801, Carey wrote to Fuller: "It has been the custom of the Moravians to give new Names to those who were converted from the Heathens. We had some consultations about it. I opposed it because I thought there was no connection between baptism and giving names but principally because it does [sic] appear to have been the primitive practice to change the names of those

---

51 Spangenberg, *Instructions for the Members of the Unitas Fratrum*, 8.

52 Spangenberg, *Instructions for the Members of the Unitas Fratrum*, 12.

53 Spangenberg, *Instructions for the Members of the Unitas Fratrum*, 16.

54 Entry for Friday, June 21, 1799, in Ward, *William Ward's Missionary Journal*, 18.

who believed."⁵⁵

There are other differences. Both documents mention the importance of the spiritual development of the individual missionary, but the *Instructions* dedicates more space to the subject. Unlike the *SFA*, the Instructions provides detailed policies for handling conflict, including procedures for appealing to a higher authority.⁵⁶ The *Instructions* also provides Moravians with a specific procedure for brethren who feel the call to be a missionary. Perhaps the *SFA* does not because it is a covenant between missionaries already on the field.⁵⁷ Again, unlike the *SFA*, the *Instructions* advises those who need to return from the field. In keeping with this concern for missionaries, the *Instructions* offers counsel on how to care for the missionaries' health, diet, and even emotional well-being,

> *If* a person be like the prophet Jonah, who wished to die, because the sun shone hot upon his head that he fainted, he can incur a disorder. For if he is weary of life on account of the hardships, which are inevitable in hot climates, and does not, through grace, recollect himself, it may be attended with painful consequences. It is indisputable, that such a melancholy, which may befall a Brother or Sister (but which one must not yield to, and may be freed from, by taking shelter in Jesus), is much more dangerous than an inflammatory fever.⁵⁸

Specific directives are given in the *Instructions* for regular reporting from the field,⁵⁹ and missionaries are advised to keep journals of their lives and work.⁶⁰ The *SFA* does not mention this, but it became the practice of the Serampore missionaries. Like the *SFA*, the *Instructions* urges the brethren to "avoid all disputations about the rights of kings and princes to one or another country."⁶¹ One of the most significant differences between the *Instructions* and the *SFA* is that the *Instructions* do not contain any concrete plans. In contrast, the *SFA* outlines initial plans for church planting, translation work, and education.

The *SFA* is also considerably shorter than the *Instructions*. Many of the differences are explained by the different purposes of the two documents. The *Instructions* was meant to provide a general manual for Moravian missionaries worldwide. The *Form of Agreement* was a covenant between the Serampore missionaries, binding them to particular theological presuppositions and missionary practices on a specific field.

Conclusion

On his voyage to India in 1799, reflecting on the Moravians' example, William Ward wrote in his journal, "I feel towards the first Greenland Missionaries a most lively affection ... Their testimony of the blood of Immanuel will I trust be mine."⁶² The connection would be

---

55 Carey to Fuller, Aug 4, 1801, in Carter, ed., *Journal and Selected Letters of William Carey*, 173.

56 Spangenberg, *Instructions for the Members of the Unitas Fratrum*, 43.

57 Spangenberg, *Instructions for the Members of the Unitas Fratrum*, 6.

58 Spangenberg, *Instructions for the Members of the Unitas Fratrum*, 49–50.

59 Spangenberg, *Instructions for the Members of the Unitas Fratrum*, 43.

60 Spangenberg, *Instructions for the Members of the Unitas Fratrum*, 51.

61 Spangenberg, *Instructions for the Members of the Unitas Fratrum*, 44.

62 Entry for June 16, 1799, in Ward, *William Ward's Missionary Journal*, 17.

more direct than Ward could imagine. When the Moravians left Serampore in 1777, they believed their mission had failed. However, in December of 1800, when the Baptist missionaries baptized their first Hindu convert, Krishna Pal (1764–1822), they reported he had first heard the gospel from the Moravian Johannes Grassman while doing carpentry work.[63] The Serampore missionaries could have expected no more evident confirmation of Christian Latrobe's statement regarding the Moravian missionary experience: "They soon found that 'to know nothing among them save Jesus & him crucified' was the right way; the Word of the Cross, proved the power of God unto Salvation, and every other good thing followed."[64]

---

[63] Potts, *British Baptist Missionaries*, 35; Carey, *William Carey*, 194.

[64] Whelan, ed., *Baptist Autographs*, 65.

Texts & Documents

"The Form of Agreement (1805)"[1]
William Ward

Respecting the great principles upon which the brethren of the Mission at Serampore think it their duty to act in the work of instructing the heathen. Agreed upon at a meeting of the Brethren at Serampore, on Monday, October 7, 1805.

The Redeemer, in planting us in this heathen nation, rather than in any other, has imposed upon us the cultivation of peculiar qualifications. We are firmly persuaded that Paul might plant and Apollos water, in vain, in any part of the world, did not God give the increase. We are sure that only those who are ordained to eternal life will believe, and that God alone can add to the Church such as shall be saved. Nevertheless we cannot but observe with admiration that Paul, the great champion for the glorious doctrines of free and sovereign grace, was the most conspicuous for his personal zeal in the work of persuading men to be reconciled to God. In this respect he is a noble example for our imitation. Our Lord intimated to those of His apostles who were fishermen, that he would make them fishers of men, intimating that in all weathers, and amidst every disappointment, they were to aim at drawing men to the shores of eternal life. Solomon says, "He that winneth souls is wise," implying, no doubt, that the work of gaining over men to the side of God was to be done by winning methods, and that it required the greatest wisdom to do it with success. Upon these points, we think it right to fix our serious and abiding attention.

1. In order to be prepared for our great and solemn work, it is absolutely necessary that we set an infinite value upon immortal souls; that we often endeavour to affect our minds with the dreadful loss sustained by an unconverted soul launched into eternity. It becomes us to fix in our minds the awful doctrine of eternal punishment, and to realise frequently the inconceivably awful condition of this vast country, lying in the arms of the wicked one. If we have not this awful sense of the value of souls, it is impossible that we can feel aright in any other part of our work, and in this case it had been better for us to have been in any other situation rather than in that of a

---

1 The original is found in *Periodical Accounts relative to the Baptist Missionary Society* 3 (Dunstable: J.W. Morris, 1805): 198–211.

missionary. Oh! may our hearts bleed over these poor idolators and may their case lie with continued weight on our minds, that we may resemble that eminent Missionary, who compared the travail of his soul, on account of the spiritual state of those committed to his charge, to the pains of childbirth. But while we thus mourn over their miserable condition, we should not be discouraged, as though their recovery were impossible. He who raised the sottish and brutalised Britons to sit in heavenly places in Christ Jesus, can raise these slaves of superstition, purify their hearts by faith, and make them worshippers of the one God in spirit and in truth. The promises are fully sufficient to remove our doubts, and to make us anticipate that not very distant period when He will famish all the gods of India, and cause these very idolaters to cast their idols to the moles and to the bats, and renounce for ever the work of their own hands.

2. It is very important that we should gain all the information we can of the snares and delusions in which these heathen are held. By this means we shall be able to converse with them in an intelligible manner. To know their modes of thinking, their habits, their propensities, their antipathies, the way in which they reason about God, sin, holiness, the way of salvation, and a future state, to be aware of the bewitching nature of their idolatrous worship, feasts, songs, etc., is of the highest consequence, if we would gain their attention to our discourse, and would avoid being barbarians to them. This knowledge may be easily obtained by conversing with sensible natives, by reading some parts of their works and by attentively observing their manners and customs.

3. It is necessary, in our intercourse with the Hindoos, that, as far as we are able, we abstain from those things which would increase their prejudices against the Gospel. Those parts of English manners which are most offensive to them should be kept out of sight as much as possible. We should also avoid every degree of cruelty to animals. Nor is it advisable at once to attack their prejudices by exhibiting with acrimony the sins of their gods; neither should we on any account do violence to their images, nor interrupt their worship. The real conquests of the Gospel are those of love: "And I, if I be lifted up, will draw all men unto me." In this respect, let us be continually fearful lest one unguarded word, or one unnecessary display of the difference betwixt us, in manners, etc., should set the natives at a greater distance from us. Paul's readiness to become all things to all men, that he might by any means save some and his disposition to abstain even from necessary comforts that he might not offend the weak, are circumstances worthy of our particular notice. This line of conduct we may be sure was founded on the wisest principles. Placed amidst a people very much like the hearers of the Apostle, in many respects, we may now perceive the solid wisdom which guided him as a missionary. The mild manners of the Moravians, and also of the Quakers, towards the North American Indians, have, in many instances, gained the affections and confidence of heathens in a wonderful manner. He who is too proud to stoop to others in order to draw them to him, though he may know that they are in many respects inferior to himself, is ill-qualified to become a Missionary. The

words of a most successful preacher of the Gospel still living, "that he would not care if the people trampled him under their feet, if he might become useful to their souls," are expressive of the very temper we should always cultivate.

4. It becomes us to watch all opportunities of doing good. A missionary would be highly culpable if he contented himself with preaching two or three times a week to those persons whom he might be able to get together into a place of worship. To carry on conversations with the natives almost every hour in the day, to go from village to village, from market to market, from one assembly to another, to talk to servants, labourers, etc., as often as opportunity offers, and to be instant in season and out of season, this is the life to which we are called in this country. We are apt to relax in these active exertions especially in a warm climate: but we shall do well always to fix in our minds that life is short, that all around us are perishing, and that we incur a dreadful woe if we proclaim not the glad tiding of salvation.

5. In preaching to the heathen, we must keep to the example of Paul, and make the great subject of our preaching, Christ the Crucified. It would be very easy for a missionary to preach nothing but truths, and that for many years together, without any well-grounded hope of becoming useful to one soul. The doctrine of Christ's expiatory death and all-sufficient merits has been, and must ever remain, the grand mean of conversion. This doctrine, and others immediately connected with it, have constantly nourished and sanctified the Church. Oh that these glorious truths may ever be the joy and strength of our own souls and then they will not fail to become the matter of our conversation to others. It was the proclaiming of these doctrines that made the Reformation from Popery in the time of Luther spread with such rapidity. It was these truths which filled the sermons of the most useful men in the eighteenth century.[2] It is a well-known fact that the most successful missionaries in the world at the present day make the atonement of Christ their continued theme. We mean the Moravians. They attribute all their success to the preaching of the death of our Saviour. So far as our experience goes in this work, we must freely acknowledge that every Hindoo among us who has been gained to Christ, has been won by the astonishing and all-constraining love exhibited in our Redeemer's propitiatory death. Oh then may we resolve to know nothing among Hindoos and Mussulmans but Christ and Him crucified.

6. It is absolutely necessary that the natives should have an entire confidence in us, and feel quite at home in our company. To gain this confidence we must on all occasions be willing to hear their complaints: we must give them the kindest advice: and we must decide upon everything brought before us in the most open, upright, and impartial manner. We ought to be easy of access, to condescend to them as much as possible, and on all occasions to treat them as our equals. All passionate behaviour will sink our

---

2 Later editions have the following sentence at this point that is not found in this original. "It was these truths [the doctrine of the cross] that filled the sermons of the modern Apostles, Whitefield, Wesley, etc., when the light of the Gospel which had been held up with such glorious effects by the Puritans was almost extinguished in England."

characters exceedingly in their estimation. All force, and everything haughty, reserved and forbidding, it becomes us ever to shun with the greatest care. We can never make sacrifices too great, when the eternal salvation of souls is the object except, indeed, we sacrifice the commands of Christ.

7. Another important part of our work is to build up, and watch over, the souls that may be gathered. In this work we shall do well to simplify our first instructions as much as possible, and to press the great principles of the Gospel upon the minds of the converts till they be thoroughly settled and grounded in the foundation of their hope towards God. We must be willing to spend some time with them daily, if possible, in this work. We must have much patience with them, though they may grow very slowly in divine knowledge. We ought also to endeavour as much as possible to form them to habits of industry, and assist them in procuring such employments as may be pursued with the least danger of temptations to evil. Here too we shall have occasion to exercise much tenderness and forbearance, knowing that industrious habits are formed with difficulty by all heathen nations.

- We ought also to remember that these persons have made no common sacrifices in renouncing their connections, their homes, their former situations and means of support, and that it will be very difficult for them to procure employment with heathen masters. In these circumstances, if we do not sympathise with them in their temporal losses for Christ, we shall be guilty of great cruelty.

- As we consider it our duty to honour the civil magistrate, and in every state and country to render him the readiest obedience, whether we be persecuted or protected, it becomes us to instruct our native brethren in the same principles. A sense of gratitude too presses this obligation upon us in a peculiar manner in return for the liberal protection we have experienced. It is equally our wisdom and our duty also to show to the civil power, that it has nothing to fear from the progress of Missions, since a real follower of Christ must resist the example of his great Master, and all the precepts the Bible contains on this subject, before he can become disloyal. Converted heathens, being brought over to the religion of their Christian Governors, if duly instructed, are much more likely to love them, and be united to them, than subjects of a different religion.

- To bear the faults of our native brethren, so as to reprove them with tenderness, and set them right in the necessity of a holy conversation, is a very necessary duty. We should remember the gross darkness in which they were so lately involved, having never had any just and adequate ideas of the evil of sin or its consequences. We should also recollect how backward human nature is in forming spiritual ideas, and entering upon a holy self-denying conversation. We ought not, therefore, even after many falls, to give up and cast away a relapsed convert while he manifests the least inclination to be washed from his filthiness.

- In walking before native converts, much care and circumspection are absolutely necessary. The falls of Christians in Europe have not such a fatal tendency as they must have in this country, because there the Word of God always commands more attention than the conduct of the most exalted Christian. But here those around us, in consequence of their little knowledge of the Scriptures, must necessarily take our conduct as a specimen of what Christ looks for in His disciples. They know only the Saviour and His doctrine as they shine forth in us.

- In conversing with the wives of native converts, and leading them on in the ways of Christ, so that they may be an ornament to the Christian cause, and make known the Gospel to the native women, we hope always to have the assistance of the females who have embarked with us in the Mission. We see that in primitive times the Apostles were very much assisted in their great work by several pious females. The great value of female help may easily be appreciated if we consider how much the Asiatic women are shut up from the men, and especially from men of another caste. It behooves us therefore, to afford to our European sisters all possible assistance in acquiring the language, that they may, in every way which Providence may open to them, become instrumental in promoting the salvation of the millions of native women who are in a great measure excluded from all opportunities of hearing the Word from the mouths of European missionaries. A European sister may do much for the cause in this respect, by promoting the holiness, and stirring up the zeal, of the female native converts. A real missionary becomes in a sense a father to his people. If he feel all the anxiety and tender solicitude of a father, all that delight in their welfare and company that a father does in the midst of his children, they will feel all that freedom with, and confidence in him which he can desire. He will be wholly unable to lead them on in a regular and happy manner, unless they can be induced to open their minds to him, and unless a sincere and mutual esteem subsist on both sides.

8. Another part of our work is the forming of our native brethren to usefulness, fostering every kind of genius, and cherishing every gift and grace in them. In this respect we can scarcely be too lavish of our attention to their improvement. It is only by means of native preachers that we can hope for the universal spread of the Gospel throughout this immense continent. Europeans are too few, and their subsistence costs too much for us ever to hope that they can possibly be the instruments of the universal diffusion of the Word amongst so many millions of souls spread over such a large portion of the habitable globe. Their incapability of bearing the intense heat of the climate in perpetual itineracies, and the heavy expenses of their journeys, not to say anything of the prejudices of the natives against the very presence of Europeans, and the great difficulty of becoming fluent in their languages, render it an absolute duty to cherish native gifts, and to send forth as many native preachers as possible. If the practice of confining the ministry of the Word to a single individual in a Church be once established amongst us, we despair of the Gospel's ever making much progress in India by our means. Let us therefore use every gift, and continually urge on our native

brethren to press upon their countrymen the glorious Gospel of the blessed God.

- Still further to strengthen the cause of Christ in this country, and as far as in our power, to give it a permanent establishment, even when the efforts of Europeans may fail, we think it our duty, as soon as possible, to advise the native brethren who may be formed into separate Churches to choose their pastors and deacons from amongst their own countrymen, that the Word may be statedly preached, and the ordinances of Christ administered, in each Church by the native minister, as much as possible without the interference of the missionary of the district who will constantly superintend their affairs, give them advice in cases of order and discipline, and correct any errors into which they may fall, and who joying and beholding their order, and the steadfastness of their faith in Christ, may direct his efforts continually to the planting of new Churches in other places, and to the spread of the Gospel throughout his district as much as in his power. By this means the unity of the missionary character will be preserved, all the missionaries will still form one body, each one moveable as the good of the cause may require; the different native Churches will also naturally learn to care and provide for their ministers, for their Church expenses, the raising of places of worship, etc., and the whole administration will assume a native aspect; by which means the inhabitants will more readily identify the cause as belonging to their own nation, and their prejudices at falling into the hands of Europeans will entirely vanish. It may be hoped too that the pastors of these Churches, and the members in general, will feel a new energy in attempting to spread the Gospel, when they shall thus freely enjoy the privileges of the Gospel amongst themselves. Under the divine blessing, if in the course of a few years a number of native Churches be thus established, from them the Word of God may sound out even to the extremities of India; and numbers of preachers being raised up and sent forth, may form a body of native missionaries, inured to the climate, acquainted with the customs, language, modes of speech, and reasoning of the inhabitants; able to become perfectly familiar with them, to enter their houses, to live upon their food, to sleep with them, or under a tree; and who may travel from one end of the country to the other almost without any expense. These Churches will be in no immediate danger of falling into errors or disorders, because the whole of their affairs will be constantly superintended by a European missionary. The advantages of this plan are so evident, that to carry it into complete effect ought to be our continued concern. That we may discharge the important obligations of watching over these infant churches when formed, and of urging them to maintain a steady discipline, to hold forth the clear and cheering light of evangelical truth in this region and shadow of death, and to walk in all respects as those who have been called out of darkness into marvellous light, we should go continually to the Source of all grace and strength; for if, to become the shepherd of one Church be a most solemn and weighty charge, what must it be to watch over a number of Churches just raised from a state of heathenism, and placed at a distance from each other.

- We have thought it our duty not to change the names of native converts, observing from Scripture that the Apostles did not change those of the first Christians turned from heathenism, as the names Epaphroditus, Phebe, Fortunatus, Sylvanus, Apollos, Hermes, Junia, Narcissus, etc., prove. Almost all these names are derived from those of heathen gods. We think the great object which divine Providence has in view in causing the Gospel to be promulgated in the world, is not the changing of the names, the dress, the food, and the innocent usages of mankind, but to produce a moral and divine change in the hearts and conduct of men. It would not be right to perpetuate the names of heathen gods amongst Christians; neither is it necessary or prudent to give a new name to every man after his conversion, as hereby the economy of families, neighbourhoods, etc., would be needlessly disturbed. In other respects we think it our duty to lead our brethren by example, by mild persuasion, and by opening and illuminating their minds in a gradual way, rather than use authoritative means. By this they learn to see the evil of a custom, and then to despise and forsake it; whereas in cases where force is used, though they may leave off that which is wrong while in our presence, yet not having seen the evil of it, they are in danger of using hypocrisy, and of doing that out of our presence which they dare not do in it.

9. It becomes us also to labour with all our might in forwarding translations of the sacred Scriptures in the languages of Hindoostan. The help which God has already afforded us in this work is a loud call to us to "go forward." So far, therefore, as God has qualified us to learn those languages which are necessary, we consider it our bounden duty to apply with unwearied assiduity in acquiring them. We consider the publication of the divine Word throughout India as an object which we ought never to give up till accomplished, looking to the Fountain of all knowledge and strength, to qualify us for this great work, and to carry us through it to the praise of His holy name.

    - It becomes us to use all assiduity in explaining and distributing the divine Word on all occasions, and by every means in our power to excite the attention and reverence of the natives towards it, as the fountain of eternal truth, and the message of salvation to men. It is our duty also to distribute, as extensively as possible, the different religious tracts which are published. Considering how much the general diffusion of the knowledge of Christ depends upon a constant and liberal distribution of the Word, and of these tracts all over the country, we should keep this continually in mind, and watch all opportunities of putting even single tracts into the hands of those persons with whom we occasionally meet. We should endeavour to ascertain where large assemblies of natives are to be found, that we may attend upon them, and gladden whole villages at once with the tidings of salvation.

    - The establishment of native free schools is also an object highly important to the future conquests of the Gospel. Of this very pleasing and interesting part of our missionary labours we should endeavour not to be unmindful. As opportunities are afforded, it becomes us to establish, visit, and encourage these institutions, and to recommend the establishment of them to other Europeans. The progress of divine light is gradual, both as it respects individuals and nations. Whatever therefore tends to increase the body of holy light in these dark regions, is as bread cast upon the waters, to be seen after many days. In many ways the progress of providential events is preparing the Hindoos for casting their idols to the moles and the bats, and for becoming a part of the chosen generation, the royal priesthood, the holy nation. Some parts of missionary labours very properly tend to the present conversion of the heathen, and others to the ushering in of the glorious period when a nation shall be born in a day. Of the latter are native free schools.

10. That which, as a means, is to fit us for the discharge of these laborious and unutterably important labours, is the being instant in prayer, and the cultivation of personal religion. Let us ever have in remembrance the examples of those who have been most eminent in the work of God. Let us often look at Brainerd in the woods of America, pouring out his very soul before God for the perishing heathen, without whose salvation nothing could make him happy. Prayer, secret, fervent, believing prayer, lies at the root of all personal godliness. A competent knowledge of the languages where a missionary lives, a mild and winning temper, and a heart given up to God in closest religion, these, these are the attainments which, more than all knowledge or all other gifts, will fit us to become the instruments of God in the great work of human redemption. Let us then ever be united in prayer at stated seasons, whatever distance may separate us, and let each one of us lay it upon his heart that we will seek to be fervent in spirit, wrestling with God, till He famish these idols, and cause the heathen to experience the blessedness that is in Christ. Finally, let us give ourselves unreservedly to this glorious cause. Let us never think that our time, our gifts, our strength, our families, or even the clothes we wear, are our own. Let us sanctify them all to God and His cause. Oh that He may sanctify us for His work. Let us for ever shut out the idea of laying up a cowrie for ourselves or our children. If we give up the resolution which was formed on the subject of private trade when we first united at Serampore, the Mission is from that hour a lost cause. A worldly spirit, quarrels, and every evil work will succeed the moment it is admitted that each brother may do something on his own account. Woe to that man who shall ever make the smallest movement toward such a measure! Let us continually watch against a worldly spirit, and cultivate a Christian indifference towards every indulgence. Rather let us bear hardness as good soldiers of Jesus Christ and endeavour to learn in every state to be content.

- If in this way we are enabled to glorify God with our bodies and spirits which are His, our wants will be His care. No private family ever enjoyed a greater portion of happiness, even in the most prosperous gale of worldly prosperity, than we have done since we resolved to have all things in common and that no one should pursue business for his own exclusive advantage. If we are enabled to persevere in the same principles, we may hope that multitudes of converted souls will have reason to bless God to all eternity for sending His Gospel into this country.

- To keep these ideas alive in our minds, we resolve that this agreement shall be read publicly, at every station, at our three annual meetings, viz. on the first Lord's day in January, in May and October.

William Carey
Joshua Marshman
William Ward
John Chamberlain
Richard Mardon
John Biss
William Moore
Joshua Rowe
Felix Carey

Mission House, Serampore

William Ward Bibliography

Drawn up by Caleb Hawkins, Landen Llamas, Joshua Sherrell, & Matthew Stewart

---

Hein, Norvin. "Early Protestant Views of Hinduism: 1600–1825." Paper presented at the third Biennial Meeting of the Association of Professors of Mission, Evangelical Theological Seminary, 1956.

Mani, Lata. *Contentious Traditions: The Debate on Sati in Colonial India*. Berkeley, CA: University of California Press, 1998.

Marshman, John Clark. *The Life and Times of Carey, Marshman, and Ward, Embracing the History of the Serampore Mission*, 2 vols. London: Longman, Brown, Green, Longmans & Roberts 1859.

Memoir of the Rev. William Ward. One of the Serampore Missionaries. Philadelphia, PA: American Sunday-School Union, 1835.

Pennington, Brian K. *Was Hinduism Invented?: Britons, Indians, and the Colonial Construction of Religion*. Oxford: Oxford University Press, 2008.

_____. "Reverend William Ward and His Legacy for Christian (Mis)perception of Hinduism." *Hindu-Christian Studies Bulletin* 13.6 (2000): 5–11.

Peucker, Paul. "The Moravians." In *The Oxford Handbook of Early Evangelicalism*. Edited by Jonathan Yeager, 117–153. Oxford: Oxford University Press, 2022.

Potts, E. Daniel. *British Baptist Missionaries in India*. Cambridge University Press, 1967.

_____. "The Baptist Missionaries of Serampore and the Government of India 1792–1813." *Journal of Ecclesiastical History* 15.2 (1964): 229–246.

_____. "'I throw away the guns to preserve the ship': A Note on the Serampore Trio." *Baptist Quarterly* 20.3 (1963): 115–117.

_____. "William Ward's Missionary Journal." *Baptist Quarterly* 25.3 (1973): 111–114.

_____. "William Ward: The Making of a Missionary in the 18th Century." In *Bicentenary*

  Volume: *William Carey's Arrival in India 1793-1993, Serampore College 1818-1993*, 27–34, Serampore: Serampore College, 1993.

Reynolds, Matthew. "The Spirituality of William Ward." PhD diss., The Southern Baptist Theological Seminary, 2019.

Smith, A. Christopher. "A Tale of Many Models: The Missiological Significance of the Serampore Trio." *Missiology* 20 (1992): 479-500.

———. "Echoes of the Protestant Reformation in Baptist Serampore, 1800-1855." *Baptist Review of Theology* 6.1 (1996): 28-61.

———. "Mythology and Missiology: A Methodological Approach to the Pre-Victorian Mission of the Serampore Trio." *International Review of Mission* 83.330 (1994): 451-475.

———. "The Edinburgh Connection: Between the Serampore Mission and Western Missiology." *Missiology* 18 (1990): 185-209.

———. "William Ward, Radical Reform, and Missions in the 1790s." *American Baptist Quarterly* 10.3 (1991): 218–244.

———. "The Legacy of William Ward and Joshua and Hannah Marshman." *International Bulletin of Missionary Research* 23 (1999): 120-129.

———. "William Ward (1769–1823)." In *The British Particular Baptists 1638–1910*. Edited by Michael A. G. Haykin, 2:254–271. Springfield, MO: Particular Baptist Press, 2000.

———. "The Protégé of Erasmus and Luther in Heroic Serampore," *Indian Journal of Theology* 37.1 (1995): 15–44.

———. *The Serampore Mission Enterprise*. Bangalore: Centre for Contemporary Christianity, 2006.

———. *The Serampore Mission Press*. Bangalore: Centre for Contemporary Christianity, 2006.

Stanley, Brian, ed. *Christian Missions and the Enlightenment*. Grand Rapids, MI: Eerdmans, 2001.

———. *The History of the Baptist Missionary Society 1792-1992*. Edinburgh: T&T Clark, 1992.

Stennett, Samuel. *Memoirs of the Life of the Rev. William Ward*. London: J. Haddon, 1825.

"The Serampore Form of Agreement." *Baptist Quarterly* 12.5 (January 1947): 125–138.

Thompson, David. "Baptists in the Eighteenth Century: Relations with Other Christians." In *Challenge and Change: English Baptist Life in the Eighteenth Century*. Edited by Stephen Copson and Peter J. Morden, 259–280. Didcot: Baptist Historical Society, 2017.

Ward, William. *Account of the Writings, Religion, and Manners of the Hindoos: Including Translations from their Principal Works in Four Volumes.* Serampore: Mission Press, 1811.

_____. *Extracts from An Account of the Writings, Religion, and Manners of the Hindoos, Including Translations from their Principal Works. In Four Volumes Quarto. No. 1. Modes of Self Torture; No. 2 Burning of Women; No. 3 Destruction of Infants; No. 4 Account of the Sikhs.* London: J. Haddon, 1813.

_____. *A View of the History, Literature, and Mythology of the Hindoos: Including a Minute Description of their Manners and Customs, and Translations from their Principal Works.* In Two Volumes. Second edition. Serampore: Mission Press, 1818 [Volume 1], 1815 [Volume 2].

_____. *A View of the History, Literature, and Religion of the Hindoos: including a Minute Description of their Manners and Customs, and Translations from their Principal Works.* 4 vols. 3rd ed. London: Black, Parbury and Allen, 1817, 1820.

_____. *A View of the History, Literature, and Religion of the Hindoos: including a Minute Description of their Manners and Customs, and Translations from their Principal Works.* 3 vols. London: Kingsbury, Parbury and Allen, 1822.

_____. A View of the History, Literature, and Religion of the Hindoos: including a Minute Description of their Manners and Customs, and Translations from their Principal Works. 5th ed. Madras: J. Higginbotham, 1863.

_____. *Farewell Letters to a Few Friends In Britain And America, On Returning to Bengal, In 1821.* New York: E. Bliss and E. White, [1821].

_____. *Farewell Letters to a Few Friends in Britain and America, on Returning to Bengal in 1821.* Lexington, KY: Thomas T. Skillman, 1822.

_____. *Reflections on the Word of God, for Every Day in the Year.* London: W. Simpkin and R. Marshall, 1825.

West, J. Ryan. "Evangelizing Bengali Muslims, 1793–1813: William Carey, William Ward, and Islam." PhD diss., The Southern Baptist Theological Seminary, 2014.

Young, Brian. "Lust for Empire and Religious Hate." *History, Religion, and Culture: British Intellectual History 1750–1950*, ed. Stefan Collini, Richard Whitmore, and Brian Young, 91-111. Cambridge: Cambridge University Press, 2000.

www.ingramcontent.com/pod-product-compliance
Lightning Source LLC
Chambersburg PA
CBHW030558080526
44585CB00012B/421